STEP-BY-STEP COOKING

ITALIAN · MEXICAN & CHINESE

RECIPES

Publications International, Ltd.

Chihuahua Cheese is a registered trademark of V & V Food Products, Inc.

ISBN: 0-7853-0898-9

Pictured on the front cover: Homemade Pizza *(page 53)*, Pork Burritos *(page 112)* and Chicken Chow Mein *(page 200)*.
Pictured on the back cover: Four-Meat Ravioli *(page 26)*, Chicken Enchiladas *(page 100)* and Mu Shu Pork *(page 192)*.

8 7 6 5 4 3 2 1

Manufactured in the U.S.A.

CONTENTS

Cannoli Pastries *(page 73)*.

Spicy Beef Tacos *(page 110)*

Mongolian Lamb *(page 182)*

STEP-BY-STEP COOKING

ITALIAN

Fettuccine alla Carbonara *(page 24)*

CLASS NOTES

In the last decade, Italian cuisine has gone from the usual spaghetti and meatballs to becoming a favorite in America's kitchens with diverse dishes like tortellini in cream sauce and seafood marinara. In fact, Americans eat more than 4 billion pounds of pasta each year. That comes to more than 17 pounds per person. With pasta popularity at an all time high, more than 150 different shapes are available!

But Italian food is clearly more than just pasta. A true Italian meal is very different from the single, large plate of pasta many of us associate with Italian cooking. In Italy, there is a series of courses rather than a main course as we know it. *Antipasto,* which literally translated means "before the pasta," is the appetizer course and can be served either hot or cold. Soup may sometimes follow or replace the antipasto. The next course—*I Primi* or first course—usually consists of a pasta dish. *I Secondi* is the second course and features meat, poultry or fish. The pasta and meat courses are sometimes combined. The salad course or *Insalata* is served after the main portion of the meal to perk up tired tastebuds. *I Dolci*, which translates to "the sweets," is the dessert course and is usually served with an espresso or cappuccino.

The recipes in this publication include many traditional dishes of Italy and illustrate the variety of this delicious cuisine. Using authentic ingredients and cooking techniques, *Step-by-Step Italian* shows even the novice cook how to achieve great results with easy step-by-step instructions and helpful how-to photographs.

COOKING PASTA

Dry Pasta: For every pound of dry pasta, bring 4 to 6 quarts of water to a full, rolling boil. Add 2 teaspoons salt, if desired. Gradually add pasta, allowing water to return to a boil. The boiling water helps circulate the pasta so that it cooks evenly. Stir frequently to prevent the pasta from sticking. Begin testing for doneness after 5 minutes of cooking. Pasta that is "al dente"—meaning "to the tooth"—is tender, yet firm. Draining the pasta as soon as it is done stops the cooking action and helps prevent overcooking. For best results, toss the pasta with sauce immediately after draining and serve within minutes. If the sauce is not ready, toss the pasta with some butter or oil to prevent it from becoming sticky. Pasta in its dry, uncooked form can be stored almost indefinitely in a cool dry place.

Fresh Pasta: Homemade pasta takes less time to cook than dry pasta. Cook fresh pasta in the same manner as dry, except begin testing for doneness after 2 minutes. Many of the recipes in *Step-by-Step Italian* show you how to make homemade pasta. Making pasta is fun and easy, but when time is short, dry pasta is a good substitute. What's important is that the pasta is never overcooked. Fresh pasta will last several weeks in the refrigerator or can be frozen for up to 1 month.

EQUIPMENT

Pastry Board: A slab made of marble or granite that is well suited for rolling dough and pastry because it is smooth and stays cool. A floured countertop or acrylic cutting board can also be used.

Pasta Machine: Pasta machines with hand-turned rollers are very useful in kneading and rolling pasta dough. Cutting attachments (fettuccine and angel hair are usually included) help to cut pasta evenly. Electric machines also mix the dough; however, the pasta usually lacks the resilience of hand-worked dough and the machines are expensive. Methods of making pasta by hand are also included in this publication.

Pastry Wheel: A straight or scalloped wheel with a handle that speeds the cutting of pastry or pasta shapes, such as ravioli. A sharp utility knife or pizza cutter can be substituted.

ITALIAN INGREDIENTS

These ingredients are normally available in Italian groceries. Many can be found in supermarkets and gourmet food stores.

Arborio Rice: Italian-grown short-grain rice that has large, plump grains with a delicious nutty taste. Arborio rice is traditionally used for risotto dishes because its high starch content produces a creamy texture and it can absorb more liquid than regular- or long-grain rice.

Cannellini Beans: Large, white Italian kidney beans available both in dry and canned forms. Dried beans need to be soaked in water several hours or overnight to rehydrate before cooking; canned beans should be rinsed and drained to freshen the beans. Cannellini beans are often used in Italian soups, such as Minestrone. Great Northern beans make a good substitute.

Capers: Flower buds of a bush native to the Mediterranean. The buds are sun-dried, then pickled in a vinegar brine. Capers should be rinsed and drained before using to remove excess salt.

Eggplant: A cousin of the tomato, the eggplant is actually a fruit, though commonly thought of as a vegetable. Eggplants come in various shapes and sizes and their color can vary from deep purple to creamy ivory. However, these varieties are similar in taste and should be salted to remove their bitter flavor. Choose firm, unblemished eggplants with a smooth, glossy skin. They should feel heavy for their size. Store in a cool, dry place and use within a day or two of the purchase date. Do not cut eggplants in advance as the flesh rapidly becomes discolored.

Fennel: An anise-flavored, bulb-shaped vegetable with celerylike stems and feathery leaves. Both the base and stems can be eaten raw in salads or sautéed, and the seeds and leaves can be used for seasoning food. Purchase clean, crisp bulbs with no sign of browning and greenery should be a fresh bright color. Store in the refrigerator, tightly wrapped in a plastic bag, for up to 5 days.

Hazelnuts (also called Filberts): Wild nuts that grow in clusters on the hazel tree. Italy is the leading producer of hazelnuts. For best results, remove the bitter brown skin that covers the nuts. Store in an airtight container in a cool, dry place for up to 1 month or freeze for up to 1 year.

Italian Plum Tomatoes: A flavorful egg-shaped tomato that comes in red and yellow varieties. As with other tomatoes, they are very perishable. Choose firm tomatoes that are fragrant and free of blemishes. Ripe tomatoes should be stored at room temperature and used within a few days. Canned tomatoes are a good substitute when fresh ones are out of season.

Mascarpone Cheese: This buttery-rich double- to triple-cream cheese made with cow's milk is the creamiest of the Italian cheeses. When purchasing cheese, check the expiration date; store covered in the refrigerator.

Olive Oil: Extracted oil from tree-ripened olives used for both salads and cooking. Olive oils are graded by the level of acidity they contain. The best are cold-pressed and produce a low level of acidity. The highest grade is extra virgin olive oil, which contains a maximum of 1 percent acidity. Virgin olive oil contains up to a 3 ½ percent acidity level, and pure olive oil is a blend of virgin olive oil and refined residue. Olive oil does not improve with age; exposure to air and heat turns oil rancid. Store olive oil in a cool, dark place for up to 6 months or refrigerate for up to 1 year. Olive oil becomes cloudy when chilled; bring chilled olive oil to room temperature before using.

Pancetta: Italian bacon that is cured with salt and spices, but not smoked. It is slightly salty, comes in a sausagelike roll and is used to flavor sauces, pasta dishes and meats. Pancetta can be tightly wrapped and refrigerated for up to 3 weeks or frozen for up to 6 months.

Parmesan Cheese: A hard, dry cheese made from skimmed cow's milk. This cheese has a straw-colored interior with a rich, sharp flavor. The imported Italian Parmigiano-Reggiano has been aged at least 2 years, whereas domestic renditions are only aged 14 months. Parmesan cheese is primarily used for grating. While pre-grated cheese is available, it does not compare with freshly grated. Store Parmesan cheese pieces loosely in plastic and refrigerate for up to 1 week. Refrigerate freshly grated Parmesan cheese in an airtight container for up to 1 week.

Pine Nuts (also called Pignolias): These nuts are inside pine cones. Italian pine nuts come from the stone pine tree. Pine nuts have a light, delicate flavor and are a well known ingredient in the classic Italian pesto sauce. Store in an airtight container in the refrigerator for up to 3 months or freeze for up to 9 months.

Prosciutto: The Italian word for "ham," prosciutto is seasoned, salt-cured and air-dried (not smoked). Although the imported Parma can now be purchased in America, the less expensive domestic prosciutto is a good substitute. It is usually sold in very thin slices and eaten as a first course with melon slices and figs. It also can be added at the last minute to cooked foods, such as pasta and vegetables. Wrap tightly and refrigerate slices for up to 3 days or freeze for up to 1 month.

Radicchio: Mainly used as a salad green, this red-leafed Italian chicory has burgundy red leaves with white ribs. It grows in a small, loose head and has tender, but firm leaves. Radicchio has a slightly bitter flavor. Choose crisp heads with no sign of browning; refrigerate in a plastic bag for up to 1 week. It may also be grilled, sautéed or baked.

Ricotta Cheese: A white, moist cheese with a slightly sweet flavor. It is rich, fresh and slightly grainy, but smoother than cottage cheese. Ricotta, which translated means "recooked," is made from heating the whey from another cooked cheese, such as mozzarella or provolone. Ricotta cheese is often used in lasagna and manicotti. Cottage cheese makes a good substitute, but with creamier results. When purchasing cheese, check the expiration date; store tightly covered in the refrigerator.

Venetian Canapés

12 slices firm white bread
 5 tablespoons butter or
   margarine, divided
 2 tablespoons all-purpose flour
¹/₂ cup milk
 3 ounces fresh mushrooms (about
   9 medium), finely chopped
 6 tablespoons grated Parmesan
   cheese, divided
 2 teaspoons anchovy paste
¹/₄ teaspoon salt
¹/₈ teaspoon black pepper
   Green and ripe olive slices, red
   and green bell pepper strips
   and rolled anchovy fillets for
   garnish

1. Preheat oven to 350°F. Cut circles out of bread slices with 2-inch round cutter. Melt 3 tablespoons butter in small saucepan. Brush both sides of bread circles lightly with butter. Bake bread circles on ungreased baking sheet 5 to 6 minutes per side until golden. Remove to wire rack. Cool completely. *Increase oven temperature to 425°F.*

2. Melt remaining 2 tablespoons butter in same small saucepan. Stir in flour; cook and stir over medium heat until bubbly. Whisk in milk; cook and stir 1 minute or until sauce thickens and bubbles. (Sauce will be very thick.) Place mushrooms in large bowl; stir in sauce, 3 tablespoons cheese, anchovy paste, salt and black pepper until well blended.

3. Spread heaping teaspoonful mushroom mixture on top of each toast round; place on ungreased baking sheet. Sprinkle remaining 3 tablespoons cheese over canapés, dividing evenly. Garnish, if desired.

4. Bake 5 to 7 minutes until tops are light brown. Serve warm.

Makes 8 to 10 servings (about 2 dozen)

Step 1. Brushing bread circles with butter.

Step 2. Stirring thickened sauce into mushrooms.

Step 3. Spreading mushroom mixture on toast rounds.

Mediterranean Frittata

¼ cup olive oil
 5 small yellow onions, thinly
 sliced
 1 can (14½ ounces) whole peeled
 tomatoes, drained and
 chopped
¼ pound prosciutto or cooked
 ham, chopped
¼ cup grated Parmesan cheese
 2 tablespoons chopped fresh
 parsley
½ teaspoon dried marjoram
 leaves, crushed
¼ teaspoon dried basil leaves,
 crushed
¼ teaspoon salt
 Generous dash freshly ground
 black pepper
 6 eggs
 2 tablespoons butter or
 margarine
 Italian parsley leaves for
 garnish

1. Heat oil in medium skillet over medium-high heat. Cook and stir onions in hot oil 6 to 8 minutes until soft and golden. Add tomatoes. Cook and stir over medium heat 5 minutes. Remove tomatoes and onions to large bowl with slotted spoon; discard drippings. Cool tomato-onion mixture to room temperature.

2. Stir prosciutto, cheese, parsley, marjoram, basil, salt and pepper into cooled tomato-onion mixture. Whisk eggs in small bowl; stir into prosciutto mixture.

3. Preheat broiler. Heat butter in large *broilerproof* skillet over medium heat until melted and bubbly; reduce heat to low.

4. Add egg mixture to skillet, spreading evenly. Cook over low heat 8 to 10 minutes until all but top ¼ inch of egg mixture is set; shake pan gently to test. *Do not stir.*

5. Broil egg mixture about 4 inches from heat 1 to 2 minutes until top of egg mixture is set. (Do not brown or frittata will be dry.) Frittata can be served hot, at room temperature or cold. To serve, cut into wedges. Garnish, if desired.   *Makes 6 to 8 appetizer servings*

Step 1. Stirring tomatoes into onion mixture.

Step 2. Stirring eggs into prosciutto mixture.

Step 4. Spreading egg mixture evenly into skillet.

Antipasto with Marinated Mushrooms

**1 recipe Marinated Mushrooms
(page 14)
4 teaspoons red wine vinegar
1 clove garlic, minced
1/2 teaspoon dried basil leaves,
crushed
1/2 teaspoon dried oregano leaves,
crushed
Generous dash freshly ground
black pepper
1/4 cup olive oil
4 ounces mozzarella cheese, cut
into 1/2-inch cubes
4 ounces prosciutto or cooked
ham, thinly sliced
4 ounces Provolone cheese, cut
into 2-inch sticks
1 jar (10 ounces) pepperoncini
peppers, drained
8 ounces hard salami, thinly
sliced
2 jars (6 ounces *each*) marinated
artichoke hearts, drained
1 can (6 ounces) pitted ripe olives,
drained
Lettuce leaves (optional)
Fresh basil leaves and chives for
garnish**

1. Prepare Marinated Mushrooms; set aside.

2. Combine vinegar, garlic, basil, oregano and black pepper in small bowl. Add oil in slow steady stream, whisking until oil is thoroughly blended. Add mozzarella cubes; stir to coat.

3. Marinate, covered, in refrigerator at least 2 hours.

4. Wrap 1/2 of prosciutto slices around Provolone sticks; roll up remaining slices separately.

5. Drain mozzarella cubes; reserve marinade.

6. Arrange mozzarella cubes, prosciutto-wrapped Provolone sticks, prosciutto rolls, marinated mushrooms, pepperoncini, salami, artichoke hearts and olives on large platter lined with lettuce, if desired.

7. Drizzle reserved marinade over pepperoncini, artichoke hearts and olives. Garnish, if desired. Serve with small forks or wooden toothpicks.

Makes 6 to 8 servings

continued on page 14

Step 2. Whisking oil into vinegar mixture.

Step 4. Wrapping prosciutto around Provolone sticks.

Antipasto with Marinated Mushrooms, continued

Marinated Mushrooms

3 tablespoons lemon juice
2 tablespoons chopped fresh parsley
$\frac{1}{2}$ teaspoon salt
$\frac{1}{4}$ teaspoon dried tarragon leaves, crushed
Generous dash freshly ground black pepper
$\frac{1}{2}$ cup olive oil
1 clove garlic
$\frac{1}{2}$ pound small or medium fresh mushrooms

1. To make marinade, combine lemon juice, parsley, salt, tarragon and pepper in medium bowl. Add oil in slow steady stream, whisking until oil is thoroughly blended.

2. Lightly crush garlic with flat side of chef's knife or mallet.

3. Spear garlic with small wooden toothpick and add to marinade.

4. Slice stems from mushrooms; reserve stems for another use. Wipe mushroom caps clean with damp kitchen towel.

5. Add mushrooms to marinade; mix well. Marinate, covered, in refrigerator 4 hours or overnight, stirring occasionally.

6. To serve, remove and discard garlic. Serve mushrooms on antipasto tray or as relish. Or, add mushrooms to tossed green salad, using marinade as dressing.   *Makes about 2 cups*

Marinated Mushrooms: Step 1.
Whisking oil into lemon juice mixture.

Marinated Mushrooms: Step 2.
Crushing garlic.

Marinated Mushrooms: Step 4.
Cleaning mushrooms.

Cioppino

6 to 8 hard-shell clams
1 quart *plus* 2 tablespoons water, divided
1 cup dry white wine
2 onions, thinly sliced
1 rib celery, chopped
3 sprigs parsley
1 bay leaf
³/₄ pound ocean perch or snapper fillets
1 can (14¹/₂ ounces) whole peeled tomatoes, undrained
1 tablespoon tomato paste
1 clove garlic, minced
1 teaspoon dried oregano leaves, crushed
1 teaspoon salt
¹/₂ teaspoon sugar
¹/₈ teaspoon pepper
2 large ripe tomatoes
2 large potatoes
1 pound fresh halibut or haddock fillets
¹/₂ pound fresh medium shrimp
2 tablespoons chopped fresh parsley
Celery leaves for garnish

1. Scrub clams with stiff brush under cold running water. Soak clams in large bowl of cold salt water 30 minutes. (Use ¹/₃ cup salt dissolved in 1 gallon of water.) Remove clams with slotted spoon; discard water.

2. Repeat soaking 2 more times.

3. To make fish stock, combine 1 quart water, wine, onions, celery, parsley sprigs and bay leaf in 6-quart stockpot or Dutch oven. Bring to a boil over high heat; reduce heat to low. Add perch; uncover and gently simmer 20 minutes.

4. Strain fish stock through sieve into large bowl. Remove perch to plate with slotted spatula; set aside. Discard onions, celery, parsley sprigs and bay leaf.

5. Return stock to stockpot; press canned tomatoes and juice through sieve into stockpot. Discard seeds. Stir in tomato paste, garlic, oregano, salt, sugar and pepper. Simmer, uncovered, over medium-low heat 20 minutes.

continued on page 16

Step 1. Scrubbing clams.

Step 3. Simmering fish stock.

Step 4. Straining fish stock.

Cioppino, continued

6. Combine clams and remaining 2 tablespoons water in large stockpot or saucepan. Cover and cook over medium heat 5 to 10 minutes until clams open; remove clams immediately with metal tongs as they open.

7. Discard any clams with unopened shells. Rinse clams; set aside.

8. Cut fresh tomatoes in half. Remove stems and seeds; discard. Coarsely chop tomatoes.

9. Peel potatoes; cut into ³/₄-inch cubes. Skin halibut; cut into 1¹/₂ × 1-inch pieces.

10. Add fresh tomatoes, potatoes and halibut to soup mixture in stockpot. Bring to a boil over high heat; reduce heat to medium-low. Cover and cook 12 to 15 minutes until potatoes are fork tender.

11. Remove shells from shrimp under cold running water. To devein, cut shallow slit down back of shrimp; pull out and discard vein. Add shrimp to soup mixture in stockpot.

12. Cook over medium heat 1 to 2 minutes just until shrimp turn opaque and are cooked through.

13. Flake reserved perch with fork; stir perch, reserved clams and chopped parsley into soup. Garnish, if desired. Serve immediately.

Makes 6 to 8 servings (about 10 cups)

Step 6. Removing opened clams.

Step 8. Seeding tomatoes.

Step 11. Deveining shrimp.

Classic Meatball Soup

2 pounds beef bones
3 ribs celery
2 carrots
1 medium onion, cut in half
1 bay leaf
6 cups cold water
1 egg
4 tablespoons chopped fresh
    parsley, divided
1 teaspoon salt, divided
$\frac{1}{2}$ teaspoon dried marjoram
    leaves, crushed
$\frac{1}{4}$ teaspoon pepper, divided
$\frac{1}{2}$ cup soft fresh bread crumbs
$\frac{1}{4}$ cup grated Parmesan cheese
1 pound ground beef
1 can (14$\frac{1}{2}$ ounces) whole peeled
    tomatoes, undrained
$\frac{1}{2}$ cup uncooked rotini or small
    macaroni

1. To make stock, rinse bones. Combine bones, celery, carrots, onion and bay leaf in 6-quart stockpot. Add water. Bring to a boil; reduce heat to low. Cover partially and simmer 1 hour, skimming foam occasionally.

2. Preheat oven to 400°F. Spray 13 × 9-inch baking pan with nonstick cooking spray. Combine egg, 3 tablespoons parsley, $\frac{1}{2}$ teaspoon salt, marjoram and $\frac{1}{8}$ teaspoon pepper in medium bowl; whisk lightly. Stir in bread crumbs and cheese. Add beef; mix well. Place meat mixture on cutting board; pat evenly into 1-inch-thick square. With sharp knife, cut meat into 1-inch squares; shape each square into a ball. Place meatballs in prepared pan; bake 20 to 25 minutes until brown on all sides and cooked through, turning occasionally. Drain on paper towels.

3. Strain stock through sieve into medium bowl. Slice celery and carrots; set aside. Discard bones, onion and bay leaf. To degrease stock, let stand 5 minutes to allow fat to rise. Holding paper towel, quickly pull across *surface only*, allowing towel to absorb fat. Discard. Repeat with clean paper towels as many times as needed to remove all fat.

4. Return stock to stockpot. Drain tomatoes, reserving juice. Chop tomatoes; add to stock with juice. Bring to a boil; uncover and boil 5 minutes. Stir in rotini, remaining $\frac{1}{2}$ teaspoon salt and $\frac{1}{8}$ teaspoon pepper. Cook 6 minutes, stirring occasionally. Add reserved vegetables and meatballs. Reduce heat to medium; cook 10 minutes until hot. Stir in remaining 1 tablespoon parsley. Season to taste.

Makes 4 to 6 servings (about 7 cups)

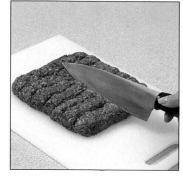

Step 2. Cutting meat into 1-inch squares.

Step 3. Degreasing stock.

Minestrone alla Milanese

¹/₄ pound green beans
2 medium zucchini
1 large potato
¹/₂ pound cabbage
¹/₃ cup olive oil
3 tablespoons butter or
   margarine
2 medium onions, chopped
3 medium carrots, coarsely
   chopped
3 ribs celery, coarsely chopped
1 clove garlic, minced
1 can (28 ounces) Italian plum
   tomatoes, undrained
3¹/₂ cups beef broth
1¹/₂ cups water
¹/₂ teaspoon salt
¹/₂ teaspoon dried basil leaves,
   crushed
¹/₄ teaspoon dried rosemary leaves,
   crushed
¹/₄ teaspoon pepper
1 bay leaf
1 can (16 ounces) cannellini beans
   Freshly grated Parmesan
   cheese (optional)

1. Trim green beans; cut into 1-inch pieces. Trim zucchini; cut into ¹/₂-inch cubes. Peel potato; cut into ³/₄-inch cubes. Coarsely shred cabbage.

2. Heat oil and butter in 6-quart stockpot or Dutch oven over medium heat. Add onions; cook and stir 6 to 8 minutes until onions are soft and golden but not brown. Stir in carrots and potato; cook and stir 5 minutes. Stir in celery and green beans; cook and stir 5 minutes. Stir in zucchini; cook and stir 3 minutes. Stir in cabbage and garlic; cook and stir 1 minute more.

3. Drain tomatoes, reserving juice. Add broth, water and reserved juice to stockpot. Chop tomatoes coarsely; add to stockpot. Stir in salt, basil, rosemary, pepper and bay leaf. Bring to a boil over high heat; reduce heat to low. Cover and simmer 1¹/₂ hours, stirring occasionally.

4. Rinse and drain cannellini beans; add beans to stockpot. Uncover and cook over medium-low heat 30 to 40 minutes more until soup thickens, stirring occasionally. Remove bay leaf. Serve with cheese.

Makes 8 to 10 servings (about 12 cups)

Step 1. Shredding cabbage with chef's knife.

Step 2. Cooking and stirring vegetables.

Step 4. Adding drained beans to stockpot.

Spaghetti alla Bolognese

2 tablespoons olive oil
1 medium onion, chopped
1 pound ground beef
$^1/_2$ small carrot, finely chopped
$^1/_2$ rib celery, finely chopped
1 cup dry white wine
$^1/_2$ cup milk
$^1/_8$ teaspoon ground nutmeg
1 can (14$^1/_2$ ounces) whole peeled
    tomatoes, undrained
1 cup beef broth
3 tablespoons tomato paste
1 teaspoon salt
1 teaspoon dried basil leaves,
    crushed
$^1/_2$ teaspoon dried thyme leaves,
    crushed
$^1/_8$ teaspoon pepper
1 bay leaf
1 pound uncooked dry spaghetti
1 cup freshly grated Parmesan
    cheese (about 3 ounces)
    Fresh thyme sprig for garnish

1. Heat oil in large skillet over medium heat. Cook and stir onion in hot oil until soft. Crumble beef into onion mixture. Brown 6 minutes, stirring to separate meat, or until meat just loses its pink color. Spoon off and discard fat.

2. Stir carrot and celery into meat mixture; cook 2 minutes over medium-high heat. Stir in wine; cook 4 to 6 minutes until wine has evaporated. Stir in milk and nutmeg; reduce heat to medium and cook 3 to 4 minutes until milk has evaporated. Remove from heat.

3. Press tomatoes and juice through sieve into meat mixture; discard seeds.

4. Stir beef broth, tomato paste, salt, basil, thyme, pepper and bay leaf into tomato-meat mixture. Bring to a boil over medium-high heat; reduce heat to low. Simmer, uncovered, 1 to 1$^1/_2$ hours until most of liquid has evaporated and sauce thickens, stirring frequently. Remove and discard bay leaf.

5. To serve, cook spaghetti in large pot of boiling salted water 8 to 12 minutes just until al dente; drain well. Combine hot spaghetti and meat sauce in serving bowl; toss lightly. Sprinkle with cheese. Garnish, if desired.

Makes 4 to 6 servings

Step 1. Browning ground beef.

Step 3. Pressing tomatoes and juice through sieve.

Step 4. Simmering tomato-meat mixture.

Fettuccine alla Carbonara

1 recipe Homemade Fettuccine
  (page 32) *or* ³/₄ pound
  uncooked dry fettuccine or
  spaghetti
4 ounces pancetta (Italian bacon)
  or lean American bacon, cut
  into ¹/₂-inch-wide strips
3 cloves garlic, halved
¹/₄ cup dry white wine
¹/₃ cup heavy or whipping cream
1 egg
1 egg yolk
²/₃ cup freshly grated Parmesan
  cheese (about 2 ounces),
  divided
  Generous dash ground white
  pepper
  Fresh oregano leaves for
  garnish

1. Prepare and cook Homemade Fettuccine or cook dry fettuccine in large pot of boiling salted water 6 to 8 minutes just until al dente; remove from heat. Drain well; return to dry pot.

2. Cook and stir pancetta and garlic in large skillet over medium-low heat 4 minutes or until pancetta is light brown. Reserve 2 tablespoons drippings in skillet with pancetta. Discard garlic and remaining drippings.

3. Add wine to pancetta mixture; cook over medium heat 3 minutes or until wine is almost evaporated. Stir in cream; cook and stir 2 minutes. Remove from heat.

4. Whisk egg and egg yolk in top of double boiler. Place top of double boiler over simmering water, adjusting heat to maintain simmer. Whisk ¹/₃ cup cheese and pepper into egg mixture; cook and stir until sauce thickens slightly.

5. Pour pancetta-cream mixture over fettuccine in pot; toss to coat. Heat over medium-low heat until heated through. Stir in egg-cheese mixture. Toss to coat evenly. Remove from heat. Serve with remaining ¹/₃ cup cheese. Garnish, if desired.

Makes 4 servings

Step 3. Stirring cream into pancetta mixture.

Step 4. Cooking sauce over double boiler to thicken.

Step 5. Tossing fettuccine with sauce.

Four-Meat Ravioli

Four-Meat Filling (page 28)
Plum Tomato Sauce (page 28)
4 cups all-purpose flour
1/4 teaspoon salt
2 eggs
1 tablespoon olive oil
2/3 to 1 cup water
1 egg yolk
1 teaspoon milk
1 tablespoon chopped fresh
    parsley
Freshly grated Parmesan
    cheese
Fresh rosemary sprig for
    garnish

1. Prepare Four-Meat Filling; refrigerate.

2. Prepare Plum Tomato Sauce; set aside.

3. For dough, mix flour and salt in large bowl. Combine 2 eggs, oil and 2/3 cup water in small bowl; whisk thoroughly. Gradually stir egg mixture into flour mixture with fork. Add enough of remaining 1/3 cup water, 1 tablespoon at a time, to form firm but pliable dough.

4. Place dough on lightly floured surface; flatten slightly. To knead dough, fold dough in half toward you and press dough away from you with heels of hands. Give dough a quarter turn and continue folding, pushing and turning. Continue kneading 5 minutes or until smooth and elastic, adding more flour to prevent sticking if necessary. Wrap dough in plastic wrap; let rest 30 minutes.

5. Unwrap dough and knead briefly (as described in step 4) on lightly floured surface; divide into 4 pieces. Using lightly floured rolling pin, roll out 1 dough piece to 1/16-inch thickness on lightly floured surface. (Keep remaining dough pieces wrapped in plastic wrap to prevent drying.) Cut dough into 4-inch-wide strips. Place teaspoonfuls of Four-Meat Filling along top half of each strip at 2-inch intervals.

6. Whisk egg yolk and milk in small bowl. Brush dough on long edge and between filling with egg-milk mixture.

continued on page 28

Step 3. Mixing egg mixture into flour with fork to form dough.

Step 4. Kneading dough.

Step 5. Placing filling on rolled out dough.

Four-Meat Ravioli, continued

7. Fold dough over filling; press firmly between filling and along long edge to seal, making sure all air has been pushed out.

8. Cut ravioli apart with fluted pastry wheel. Repeat with remaining 3 dough pieces, filling and egg-milk mixture.

9. Cook ravioli, ¼ at a time, in large pot of boiling salted water 3 to 5 minutes just until al dente. Remove with slotted spoon; drain well. Add ravioli to reserved sauce. Bring sauce and ravioli to a boil over medium-high heat; reduce heat to medium-low. Simmer, uncovered, 6 to 8 minutes until heated through. Sprinkle with parsley and cheese. Garnish, if desired. Serve immediately.

Makes 6 servings

Four-Meat Filling

**5 ounces fresh spinach, cleaned, cooked and squeezed dry
2 tablespoons butter or margarine
2 small boneless skinless chicken breast halves (about 4 ounces each), cooked
3 ounces prosciutto or cooked ham
1½ ounces hard salami
1 clove garlic
6 ounces ground beef
½ cup chopped fresh parsley
2 eggs
¼ teaspoon ground allspice
¼ teaspoon salt**

1. To steam spinach, rinse spinach thoroughly in large bowl of water; drain but do not squeeze dry. Trim and discard stems. Stack leaves; cut crosswise into coarse shreds. Place spinach in large saucepan over medium heat. Cover and steam 4 minutes or until tender, stirring occasionally. Add 2 tablespoons butter; cook and stir until butter is absorbed. Remove from pan; set aside.

2. Mince spinach, chicken, prosciutto, salami and garlic; combine in medium bowl with beef, parsley, eggs, allspice and salt. Mix well.

Plum Tomato Sauce

**⅓ cup butter or margarine
1 clove garlic, minced
1 can (28 ounces) Italian plum tomatoes, undrained
1 can (8 ounces) tomato sauce
¾ teaspoon salt
½ teaspoon ground allspice
½ teaspoon dried basil leaves, crushed
½ teaspoon dried rosemary leaves, crushed
⅛ teaspoon pepper**

1. Heat butter in large saucepan over medium heat until melted and bubbly; cook and stir garlic in hot butter 30 seconds. Press tomatoes and juice through sieve into garlic mixture; discard seeds. Stir in tomato sauce, salt, allspice, basil, rosemary and pepper.

2. Cover and simmer 30 minutes. Uncover and simmer 15 minutes more or until sauce thickens, stirring occasionally.

Step 7. Pressing dough over filling.

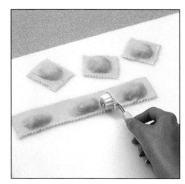

Step 8. Cutting ravioli apart with pastry wheel.

Spinach Lasagna

1 pound ground beef
¼ pound fresh mushrooms, thinly sliced
1 medium onion, chopped
1 clove garlic, minced
1 can (28 ounces) Italian plum tomatoes, undrained
1¼ teaspoons salt, divided
¾ teaspoon dried oregano leaves, crushed
¾ teaspoon dried basil leaves, crushed
¼ teaspoon pepper, divided
9 uncooked lasagna noodles
¼ cup *plus* 1 tablespoon butter or margarine, divided
¼ cup all-purpose flour
⅛ teaspoon ground nutmeg
2 cups milk
1½ cups shredded mozzarella cheese (about 6 ounces), divided
½ cup grated Parmesan cheese, divided
1 package (10 ounces) frozen chopped spinach, thawed and squeezed dry

1. For meat sauce, crumble ground beef into large skillet over medium-high heat. Brown 8 to 10 minutes, stirring to separate meat, until meat loses its pink color. Spoon off and discard fat.

2. Stir in mushrooms, onion and garlic; cook over medium heat 5 minutes or until onion is soft.

3. Press tomatoes and juice through sieve into meat mixture; discard seeds.

4. Stir in ¾ teaspoon salt, oregano, basil and ⅛ teaspoon pepper. Bring to a boil over medium-high heat; reduce heat to low. Cover and simmer 40 minutes, stirring occasionally. Uncover and simmer 15 to 20 minutes more until sauce thickens. Set aside.

5. Add lasagna noodles to large pot of boiling salted water, 1 at a time, allowing noodles to soften and fit into pot. Cook 10 minutes or just until al dente.

6. Drain noodles; rinse with cold water. Drain again; hang individually over pot rim to prevent sticking. Set aside.

Step 3. Pressing tomatoes and juice through sieve.

Step 5. Adding lasagna noodles to boiling water.

continued on page 30

Spinach Lasagna, continued

7. For cheese sauce, melt ¼ cup butter in medium saucepan over medium heat. Stir in flour, remaining ½ teaspoon salt, remaining ⅛ teaspoon pepper and nutmeg; cook and stir until bubbly. Whisk in milk; cook and stir until sauce thickens and bubbles. Cook and stir 1 minute more. Remove from heat. Stir in 1 cup mozzarella and ¼ cup Parmesan cheeses. Stir until smooth. Set aside.

8. Preheat oven to 350°F. Spread remaining 1 tablespoon butter on bottom and sides of 12 × 8-inch baking dish with waxed paper. Spread noodles in single layer on clean kitchen (not paper) towel. Pat noodles dry.

9. Arrange 3 lasagna noodles in single layer, overlapping slightly, in bottom of baking dish.

10. Top with ½ of reserved meat sauce; spread evenly. Spread ½ of reserved cheese sauce over meat sauce in even layer.

11. Repeat layers once, using 3 noodles, remaining meat sauce and remaining cheese sauce. Sprinkle spinach over cheese sauce in even layer; pat down lightly. Arrange remaining 3 lasagna noodles over spinach.

12. Mix remaining ½ cup mozzarella and remaining ¼ cup Parmesan cheeses in cup. Sprinkle cheeses evenly on top of lasagna to completely cover lasagna noodles.

13. Bake 40 minutes or until top is golden and edges are bubbly. Let lasagna stand 10 minutes before serving. Garnish as desired.

Makes 6 servings

Step 8. Greasing baking dish with butter.

Step 10. Spreading cheese sauce over meat sauce.

Step 12. Sprinkling cheeses over top of lasagna.

Classic Fettuccine Alfredo

1 recipe Homemade Fettuccine (recipe follows) *or* ³⁄₄ pound uncooked dry fettuccine
6 tablespoons unsalted butter
²⁄₃ cup heavy or whipping cream
¹⁄₂ teaspoon salt
  Generous dash ground white pepper
  Generous dash ground nutmeg
1 cup freshly grated Parmesan cheese (about 3 ounces)
2 tablespoons chopped fresh parsley
  Fresh Italian parsley sprig for garnish

1. Prepare and cook Homemade Fettuccine or cook dry fettuccine in large pot of boiling salted water 6 to 8 minutes just until al dente; remove from heat. Drain well; return to dry pot.

2. Place butter and cream in large, heavy skillet over medium-low heat. Cook and stir until butter melts and mixture bubbles. Cook and stir 2 minutes more. Stir in salt, pepper and nutmeg. Remove from heat. Gradually stir in cheese until thoroughly blended and smooth. Return briefly to heat to completely blend cheese if necessary. (Do not let sauce bubble or cheese will become lumpy and tough.)

3. Pour sauce over fettuccine in pot. Stir and toss with 2 forks over low heat 2 to 3 minutes until sauce is thickened and fettuccine is evenly coated. Sprinkle with chopped parsley. Garnish, if desired. Serve immediately.

Makes 4 servings

Step 2. Stirring cheese into sauce.

Homemade Fettuccine: Step 1. Mixing egg mixture into flour with fork to form dough.

Homemade Fettuccine

2 cups all-purpose flour
¹⁄₄ teaspoon salt
3 eggs
1 tablespoon milk
1 teaspoon olive oil

1. Combine flour and salt on pastry board, cutting board or countertop; make well in center. Whisk eggs, milk and oil in small bowl until well blended; gradually pour into well in flour mixture while mixing with fork or fingertips to form ball of dough.

continued on page 34

Classic Fettuccine Alfredo, continued

2. Place dough on lightly floured surface; flatten slightly. To knead dough, fold dough in half toward you and press dough away from you with heels of hands. Give dough a quarter turn and continue folding, pushing and turning. Continue kneading 5 minutes or until smooth and elastic, adding more flour to prevent sticking if necessary. Wrap dough in plastic wrap; let stand 15 minutes.

3. Unwrap dough and knead briefly (as described in step 2) on lightly floured surface. Using lightly floured rolling pin, roll out dough to ⅛-inch-thick circle on lightly floured surface. Gently pick up dough circle with both hands. Hold it up to the light to check for places where dough is too thick. Return to board; even out any thick spots. Let rest until dough is slightly dry but can be handled without breaking.

4. Lightly flour dough circle; roll loosely on rolling pin.

5. Slide rolling pin out; press dough roll gently with hand and cut into ¼-inch-wide strips with sharp knife. Carefully unfold strips.*

6. Cook fettuccine in large pot of boiling salted water 1 to 2 minutes just until al dente. Drain well.

Makes about ¾ pound

*Fettuccine can be dried and stored at this point. Hang fettuccine strips over pasta rack or clean broom handle covered with plastic wrap and propped between two chairs. Dry at least 3 hours; store in airtight container at room temperature up to 4 days. To serve, cook fettuccine in large pot of boiling salted water 3 to 4 minutes just until al dente. Drain well.

Homemade Fettuccine: Step 2. Kneading dough.

Homemade Fettuccine: Step 4. Rolling dough loosely on rolling pin.

Homemade Fettuccine: Step 5. Cutting dough into strips.

Homemade Angel Hair Pasta with Classic Tomato Sauces

**2 cups *plus* 2 tablespoons
  all-purpose flour**
¼ teaspoon salt
3 eggs
1 tablespoon milk
1 teaspoon olive oil
Neapolitan Sauce (page 36)
Pizzaiola Sauce (page 36)
**½ cup freshly grated Parmesan
  cheese (optional)**
**Fresh marjoram sprigs for
  garnish**

1. Place flour, salt, eggs, milk and oil in food processor; process until dough forms. Shape into ball.

2. Place dough on lightly floured surface; flatten slightly. Cut dough into 4 pieces. Wrap 3 dough pieces in plastic wrap; set aside.

3. To knead dough by pasta machine,* set rollers of pasta machine at widest setting (position 1). Feed unwrapped dough piece through flat rollers by turning handle. (Dough may crumble slightly at first but will hold together after two to three rollings.)

4. Lightly flour dough strip; fold strip into thirds. Feed through rollers again. Continue process 7 to 10 times until dough is smooth and elastic.

5. To roll out dough by machine, reduce setting to position 3. Feed dough strip through rollers. Without folding strip into thirds, repeat on positions 5 and 6. Let dough stand 5 to 10 minutes until slightly dry.

*Follow manufacturer's directions for appropriate method of rolling pasta if position settings are different. To make pasta by hand, see Homemade Fettuccine (page 32).

continued on page 36

Step 1. Processing dough.

Step 3. Kneading dough with pasta machine.

Step 4. Folding dough into thirds.

Homemade Angel Hair Pasta with Classic Tomato Sauces, continued

6. Attach handle to angel hair pasta roller and feed dough through.** Repeat kneading and rolling with reserved dough pieces.

7. Cook angel hair pasta in large pot of boiling salted water 1 to 2 minutes just until al dente; remove from heat. Drain well; divide angel hair pasta into 2 large bowls.

8. Prepare Neapolitan Sauce and Pizzaiola Sauce. Pour hot Neapolitan Sauce over ¹/₂ of angel hair pasta; toss until well coated. Pour hot Pizzaiola Sauce over remaining angel hair pasta; toss until well coated. Serve with cheese. Garnish, if desired.

Makes 4 to 6 servings

**Angel hair pasta can be dried and stored at this point. Hang pasta strips over pasta rack or clean broom handle covered with plastic wrap and propped between two chairs. (Or, twirl pasta into nests and place on clean kitchen towel.) Dry at least 3 hours; store in airtight container at room temperature up to 4 days. To serve, cook angel hair pasta in large pot of boiling salted water 3 to 4 minutes just until al dente. Drain well; proceed as directed in step 8.

Neapolitan Sauce

   2 tablespoons butter or margarine
   1 tablespoon olive oil
   1 can (28 ounces) Italian plum
      tomatoes, undrained
   1 teaspoon dried basil leaves, crushed
 ¹/₂ teaspoon salt
 ¹/₈ teaspoon pepper
   3 tablespoons chopped fresh parsley

Heat butter and oil in 2-quart saucepan over medium heat. Press tomatoes and juice through sieve into hot butter mixture; discard seeds. Stir in basil, salt and pepper. Bring to a boil over high heat; reduce heat to medium-low. Cook, uncovered, 30 to 40 minutes until sauce is reduced to 2 cups, stirring frequently. Stir in parsley.

Pizzaiola Sauce

   1 tablespoon olive oil
   2 cloves garlic
   1 can (28 ounces) Italian plum
      tomatoes, undrained
 ³/₄ teaspoon dried marjoram leaves,
      crushed
 ¹/₂ teaspoon salt
 ¹/₈ teaspoon pepper
   2 tablespoons minced fresh parsley

Heat oil in 2-quart saucepan over medium heat. Cut garlic in half. Cook and stir garlic in hot oil 2 to 3 minutes until garlic is golden but not brown. Remove and discard garlic. Press tomatoes and juice through sieve into garlic-flavored oil; discard seeds. Stir in marjoram, salt and pepper. Bring to a boil over high heat; reduce heat to medium-low. Cook, uncovered, 30 to 40 minutes until sauce is reduced to 2 cups, stirring frequently. Stir in parsley.

Step 6. Feeding dough through angel hair pasta roller.

Neapolitan Sauce: Pressing tomatoes and juice through sieve.

Pizzaiola Sauce: Cooking sauce.

Classic Pesto with Linguine

Homemade Linguine *or*
  ³/4 pound dry uncooked
  linguine, hot cooked and
  drained
2 tablespoons butter or
  margarine
¹/4 cup *plus* 1 tablespoon olive oil,
  divided
2 tablespoons pine nuts
1 cup tightly packed fresh (not
  dried) basil leaves, rinsed,
  drained and stemmed
2 cloves garlic
¹/4 teaspoon salt
¹/4 cup freshly grated Parmesan
  cheese
1¹/2 tablespoons freshly grated
  Romano cheese
  Fresh basil leaves for garnish

1. To prepare Homemade Linguine, make dough following steps 1 and 2 of Homemade Fettuccine (page 32). In step 3, roll out dough to ¹/16-inch-thick circle. In step 5, cut dough into ¹/8-inch-wide strips. Proceed as directed in step 6. Add butter to cooked and drained pasta, tossing to coat evenly.

2. To toast pine nuts, heat 1 tablespoon oil in small saucepan or skillet over medium-low heat. Add pine nuts; cook and stir 30 to 45 seconds until light brown, shaking pan constantly. Remove with slotted spoon; drain on paper towels.

3. Place toasted pine nuts, basil leaves, garlic and salt in food processor or blender. With processor running, add remaining ¹/4 cup oil in slow steady stream until evenly blended and pine nuts are finely chopped.

4. Transfer basil mixture to small bowl. Stir in Parmesan and Romano cheeses.*

5. Combine hot, buttered linguine and pesto sauce in large serving bowl; toss until well coated. Garnish, if desired. Serve immediately.
  Makes 4 servings (about ³/4 cup pesto sauce)

*Pesto sauce can be stored at this point in airtight container; pour thin layer of olive oil over pesto and cover. Refrigerate up to 1 week. Bring to room temperature. Proceed as directed in step 5.

Step 1. Cutting dough into strips.

Step 2. Toasting pine nuts.

Step 3. Adding oil through feed tube while processing.

Veal Scallopine

4 veal cutlets, cut ³⁄₈ inch thick
(about 4 ounces each)
¹⁄₄ cup butter or margarine
¹⁄₂ pound fresh mushrooms, thinly
sliced
2 tablespoons olive oil
1 small onion, finely chopped
¹⁄₄ cup dry sherry
2 teaspoons all-purpose flour
¹⁄₂ cup beef broth
¹⁄₄ teaspoon salt
¹⁄₈ teaspoon pepper
2 tablespoons heavy or whipping
cream
Fresh bay leaf and marjoram
sprigs for garnish
Hot cooked pasta (optional)

1. Pound veal with meat mallet to ¹⁄₄-inch thickness (technique on page 42). Pat dry with paper towels; set aside.

2. Heat butter in large skillet over medium heat until melted and bubbly. Cook and stir mushrooms in hot butter 3 to 4 minutes until light brown. Remove mushrooms with slotted spoon to small bowl; set aside.

3. Add oil to butter remaining in skillet; heat over medium heat. Add veal; cook 2 to 3 minutes per side until light brown. Remove veal with slotted spatula to plate; set aside.

4. Add onion to same skillet; cook and stir 2 to 3 minutes until soft. Stir sherry into onion mixture. Bring to a boil over medium-high heat; boil 15 seconds. Stir in flour; cook and stir 30 seconds. Remove from heat; stir in broth. Bring to a boil over medium heat, stirring constantly. Stir in reserved mushrooms, salt and pepper. Add reserved veal to sauce mixture; reduce heat to low. Cover and simmer 8 minutes or until veal is tender. Remove from heat.

5. Push veal to one side of skillet. Stir cream into sauce mixture; mix well. Cook over low heat until heated through. Garnish, if desired. Serve immediately with pasta.

Makes 4 servings

Step 2. Cooking mushrooms.

Step 3. Cooking veal.

Step 5. Stirring cream into sauce mixture.

Veal Parmesan

4 veal cutlets, cut ³/₈ inch thick
    (about 4 ounces each)
4 tablespoons olive oil, divided
1 small red bell pepper, finely
    chopped
1 medium onion, finely chopped
1 rib celery, finely chopped
1 clove garlic, minced
1 can (14½ ounces) whole peeled
    tomatoes, undrained and
    finely chopped
1 cup chicken broth
1 tablespoon tomato paste
1 tablespoon chopped parsley
1 teaspoon sugar
³/₄ teaspoon dried basil leaves,
    crushed
½ teaspoon salt
⅛ teaspoon ground black pepper
1 egg
¼ cup all-purpose flour
²/₃ cup fine dry bread crumbs
2 tablespoons butter or
    margarine
1½ cups shredded mozzarella
    cheese (about 6 ounces)
²/₃ cup freshly grated Parmesan
    cheese
    Fresh basil leaves for garnish
    Hot cooked pasta (optional)

1. Place each veal cutlet between sheets of waxed paper on wooden board. Pound veal with meat mallet to ¼-inch thickness. Pat dry with paper towels; set aside.

2. To make tomato sauce, heat 1 tablespoon oil in medium saucepan over medium heat. Cook and stir bell pepper, onion, celery and garlic in hot oil 5 minutes. Stir in tomatoes and juice, broth, tomato paste, parsley, sugar, dried basil, salt and black pepper. Cover and simmer over low heat 20 minutes. Uncover and cook over medium heat 20 minutes more or until sauce thickens, stirring frequently; set aside.

3. Beat egg in shallow bowl; spread flour and bread crumbs on separate plates. Dip reserved veal cutlets to coat both sides evenly, first in flour, then in egg, then in bread crumbs. Press crumb coating firmly onto veal.

4. Heat butter and 2 tablespoons oil in large skillet over medium-high heat. Add veal. Cook 3 minutes per side or until browned.

5. Preheat oven to 350°F. Remove veal with slotted spatula to ungreased 13×9-inch baking dish. Sprinkle mozzarella cheese evenly over veal. Spoon reserved tomato sauce evenly over cheese. Sprinkle Parmesan cheese over tomato sauce.

6. Drizzle remaining 1 tablespoon oil over top. Bake, uncovered, 25 minutes or until veal is tender and cheese is golden. Garnish, if desired. Serve with pasta.

Makes 4 servings

Step 1. Pounding veal to ¼-inch thickness.

Step 3. Coating veal with bread crumbs.

Step 5. Sprinkling Parmesan cheese over tomato sauce.

Chicken Cacciatore

1 broiler-fryer chicken (3 to
    3½ pounds), cut into 8 pieces
1 tablespoon olive oil
4 ounces fresh mushrooms, finely
    chopped
1 medium onion, chopped
1 clove garlic, minced
½ cup dry white wine
1½ tablespoons white wine vinegar
½ cup chicken broth
1 teaspoon dried basil leaves,
    crushed
½ teaspoon dried marjoram
    leaves, crushed
½ teaspoon salt
⅛ teaspoon pepper
1 can (14½ ounces) whole peeled
    tomatoes, undrained
8 Italian- or Greek-style black
    olives
1 tablespoon chopped fresh
    parsley
  Hot cooked pasta
  Fresh marjoram leaves for
    garnish

1. Rinse chicken; drain and pat dry with paper towels. Heat oil in large skillet over medium heat. Add chicken pieces in single layer, without crowding, to hot oil. Cook 8 minutes per side or until chicken is brown; remove chicken with slotted spatula to Dutch oven. Repeat with remaining chicken pieces; set aside.

2. Add mushrooms and onion to drippings remaining in skillet. Cook and stir over medium heat 5 minutes or until onion is soft. Add garlic; cook and stir 30 seconds. Add wine and vinegar; cook over medium-high heat 5 minutes or until liquid is almost evaporated. Stir in broth, basil, marjoram, salt and pepper. Remove from heat.

3. Press tomatoes and juice through sieve into onion mixture; discard seeds. Bring to a boil over medium-high heat; boil, uncovered, 2 minutes.

4. Pour tomato-onion mixture over chicken. Bring to a boil; reduce heat to low. Cover and simmer 25 minutes or until chicken is tender and juices run clear when pierced with fork. Remove chicken with slotted spatula to heated serving dish; keep warm.

5. Bring tomato-onion mixture to a boil over medium-high heat; boil, uncovered, 5 minutes. Cut olives in half; remove and discard pits.

6. Add olives and parsley to sauce; cook 1 minute more. Pour sauce over chicken and pasta. Garnish, if desired.

Makes 4 to 6 servings

Step 1. Cooking chicken pieces.

Step 4. Piercing chicken with fork to test for doneness.

Step 5. Pitting olives.

Classic Chicken Marsala

2 tablespoons unsalted butter
1 tablespoon vegetable oil
4 boneless skinless chicken breast halves (about 1¼ pounds total)
4 slices mozzarella cheese (1 ounce each)
12 capers, drained
4 flat anchovy fillets, drained
1 tablespoon chopped fresh parsley
1 clove garlic, minced
3 tablespoons marsala
⅔ cup heavy or whipping cream
Dash salt
Dash pepper
Hot cooked pasta (optional)

1. Heat butter and oil in large skillet over medium-high heat until melted and bubbly. Add chicken; reduce heat to medium. Cook, uncovered, 5 to 6 minutes per side until chicken is tender and golden brown. Remove chicken with slotted spatula to work surface. Top each chicken piece with 1 cheese slice, 3 capers and 1 anchovy fillet.

2. Return chicken to skillet. Sprinkle with parsley. Cover and cook over low heat 3 minutes or until cheese is semi-melted and juices from chicken run clear. Remove chicken with slotted spatula to heated serving platter; keep warm.

3. Add garlic to drippings remaining in skillet; cook and stir over medium heat 30 seconds. Stir in marsala; cook and stir 45 seconds, scraping up any brown bits in skillet.

4. Stir in cream. Cook and stir 3 minutes or until sauce thickens slightly. Stir in salt and pepper. Spoon sauce over chicken. Serve with pasta. Garnish as desired.

Makes 4 servings

Step 1. Topping chicken with cheese, capers and anchovies.

Step 2. Removing chicken with slotted spatula.

Step 3. Stirring marsala into garlic mixture.

Fish alla Milanese

¹/₃ cup *plus* **2 tablespoons olive oil, divided**
2 tablespoons lemon juice
¹/₂ teaspoon salt
Dash pepper
1 small onion, finely chopped
1 pound flounder or haddock fillets (4 to 8 pieces)
2 eggs
1 tablespoon milk
¹/₂ cup all-purpose flour
³/₄ cup fine dry unseasoned bread crumbs
¹/₄ cup *plus* 2 tablespoons butter or margarine, divided
1 clove garlic, minced
1 tablespoon chopped fresh parsley
Fresh thyme sprig for garnish
Lemon slices (optional)

1. For marinade, whisk ¹/₃ cup oil, lemon juice, salt and pepper in small bowl; stir in onion. Pour marinade into 13 × 9-inch glass baking dish.

2. Rinse fish; pat dry with paper towels. Place fish in baking dish; spoon marinade over fish to coat thoroughly. Marinate, covered, in refrigerator 1 hour, turning fish over occasionally.

3. Combine eggs and milk in shallow bowl; mix well. Spread flour and bread crumbs on separate plates. Remove fish from marinade; pat dry with paper towels. Discard marinade.

4. Dip fish to coat both sides evenly, first in flour, then in egg mixture, then in bread crumbs. Press crumb coating firmly onto fish. Place on waxed paper; refrigerate 15 minutes.

5. Heat 2 tablespoons butter and remaining 2 tablespoons oil in large skillet over medium heat until melted and bubbly; add fish. Cook 2 to 3 minutes per side until fish flakes easily with a fork and topping is light brown. Remove to heated serving plate.

6. Melt remaining ¹/₄ cup butter in medium skillet over medium heat. Add garlic. Cook 1 to 2 minutes until butter turns light brown; stir in parsley. Pour browned butter mixture over fish. Garnish, if desired. Serve immediately with lemon slices.

Makes 3 to 4 servings

Step 2. Spooning marinade over fish.

Step 4. Dipping fish in egg mixture and coating with bread crumbs.

Step 5. Flaking fish with fork to test for doneness.

Fried Calamari with Tartar Sauce

1 pound fresh or thawed frozen squid
1 egg
1 tablespoon milk
³/₄ cup fine dry unseasoned bread crumbs
Vegetable oil
Tartar Sauce (page 52)
Lemon wedges (optional)

1. To clean each squid, hold body of squid firmly in one hand. Grasp head firmly with other hand; pull head, twisting gently from side to side. (Head and contents of body should pull away in one piece.) Set aside tubular body sac.

2. Cut tentacles off head; set aside. Discard head and contents of body.

3. Grasp tip of pointed, thin, clear cartilage protruding from body; pull out and discard.

4. Rinse squid under cold running water. Peel off and discard spotted outer membrane covering body sac and fins. Pull off side fins; set aside.

5. Rinse inside of squid body thoroughly under running water. Repeat with remaining squid.

6. Cut each squid body crosswise into ¹/₄-inch rings. Cut reserved fins into thin slices. (Body rings, fins and reserved tentacles are all edible parts.) Pat pieces thoroughly dry with paper towels.

continued on page 52

Step 1. Removing head and contents of body from body sac.

Step 4. Peeling off membrane covering body sac.

Step 6. Cutting squid body into rings.

Fried Calamari with Tartar Sauce,
continued

7. Beat egg with milk in small bowl. Add squid pieces; stir to coat well. Spread bread crumbs in shallow bowl. Dip squid pieces in bread crumbs; place on plate or on waxed paper. Let stand 10 to 15 minutes before frying.

8. To deep fry squid, heat 1½ inches oil in large saucepan to 350°F. (*Caution:* Squid will pop and spatter during frying; do not stand too close to pan.) Adjust heat to maintain temperature. Fry 8 to 10 pieces of squid at a time in hot oil 45 to 60 seconds until light brown. Remove with slotted spoon; drain on paper towels. Repeat with remaining squid pieces.

9. Or, to shallow fry squid, heat about ¼ inch oil in large skillet over medium-high heat; reduce heat to medium. Add pieces of squid in single layer, without crowding, to hot oil. Cook, turning once with 2 forks, 1 minute per side or until light brown. Remove with slotted spoon; drain on paper towels. Repeat with remaining squid. (This method uses less oil but requires slightly more hand work.)

10. Serve hot with Tartar Sauce and lemon wedges. Garnish as desired.

Makes 2 to 3 servings

Tartar Sauce

1 green onion
1 tablespoon drained capers
1 small sweet gherkin or pickle
2 tablespoons chopped fresh parsley
1⅓ cups mayonnaise

1. Thinly slice green onion. Mince capers and gherkin.

2. Fold green onion, capers, gherkin and parsley into mayonnaise. Cover and refrigerate until ready to serve.

Makes about 1⅓ cups

Step 7. Coating squid with bread crumbs.

Step 8. Deep frying squid.

Step 9. Turning squid with forks when shallow frying.

Homemade Pizza

½ tablespoon active dry yeast
1 teaspoon sugar, divided
½ cup warm water
(105°F to 115°F)
1¾ cups all-purpose flour, divided
¾ teaspoon salt, divided
2 tablespoons olive oil, divided
1 can (14½ ounces) whole peeled
tomatoes, undrained
1 medium onion, chopped
1 clove garlic, minced
2 tablespoons tomato paste
1 teaspoon dried oregano leaves,
crushed
½ teaspoon dried basil leaves,
crushed
⅛ teaspoon ground black pepper
½ small red bell pepper, cored and
seeded
½ small green bell pepper, cored
and seeded
4 fresh medium mushrooms
1 can (2 ounces) flat anchovy
fillets
1¾ cups shredded mozzarella
cheese
½ cup freshly grated Parmesan
cheese (about 7 ounces)
⅓ cup pitted ripe olives, halved

1. To proof yeast, sprinkle yeast and ½ teaspoon sugar over warm water in small bowl; stir until yeast is dissolved. Let stand 5 minutes or until mixture is bubbly.*

2. Place 1½ cups flour and ¼ teaspoon salt in medium bowl; stir in yeast mixture and 1 tablespoon oil, stirring until a smooth, soft dough forms. Place dough on lightly floured surface; flatten slightly.

3. To knead dough, fold dough in half toward you and press dough away from you with heels of hands. Give dough a quarter turn and continue folding, pushing and turning. Continue kneading, using as much of remaining ¼ cup flour as needed to form a stiff, elastic dough.

4. Shape dough into a ball; place in large greased bowl. Turn to grease entire surface. Cover with clean kitchen towel and let dough rise in warm place 30 to 45 minutes until doubled in bulk.

5. Press two fingertips about ½ inch into dough. Dough is ready if indentations remain when fingers are removed.

*If yeast does not bubble, it is no longer active. Always check expiration date on yeast packet. Also, water that is too hot will kill yeast; it is best to use a thermometer.

continued on page 54

Step 1. Proofing yeast.

Step 3. Kneading dough.

Step 5. Pressing fingertips into dough to test if ready.

Homemade Pizza, continued

6. For sauce, finely chop tomatoes in can with knife, reserving juice. Heat remaining 1 tablespoon oil in medium saucepan over medium heat. Add onion; cook 5 minutes or until soft. Add garlic; cook 30 seconds more. Add tomatoes and juice, tomato paste, oregano, basil, remaining ½ teaspoon sugar, ½ teaspoon salt and black pepper. Bring to a boil over high heat; reduce heat to medium-low. Simmer, uncovered, 10 to 15 minutes until sauce thickens, stirring occasionally. Pour into small bowl; cool.

7. Punch dough down. Knead briefly (as described in step 3) on lightly floured surface to distribute air bubbles; let dough stand 5 minutes more. Flatten dough into circle on lightly floured surface. Roll out dough, starting at center and rolling to edges, into 10-inch circle. Place circle in greased 12-inch pizza pan; stretch and pat dough out to edges of pan. Cover and let stand 15 minutes.

8. Preheat oven to 450°F. Cut bell peppers into ¾-inch pieces. Trim mushroom stems; wipe clean with damp kitchen towel (technique on page 14) and thinly slice. Drain anchovies. Mix mozzarella and Parmesan cheeses in small bowl.

9. Spread sauce evenly over pizza dough.

10. Sprinkle with ⅔ of cheeses. Arrange bell peppers, mushrooms, anchovies and olives over cheeses.

11. Sprinkle remaining cheeses on top of pizza. Bake 20 minutes or until crust is golden brown. To serve, cut into wedges.   *Makes 4 to 6 servings*

Step 7. Rolling out dough.

Step 9. Spreading sauce over dough.

Tomato, Mozzarella & Basil Salad

2 tablespoons red wine vinegar
1 clove garlic, minced
½ teaspoon salt
¼ teaspoon dry mustard
   Generous dash freshly ground
   black pepper
⅓ cup olive or vegetable oil
4 Italian plum tomatoes
6 ounces mozzarella cheese
8 to 10 fresh basil leaves

1. For dressing, combine vinegar, garlic, salt, mustard and pepper in small bowl. Add oil in slow steady stream, whisking until oil is thoroughly blended (technique on page 12).

2. Slice tomatoes and cheese into ¼-inch-thick slices. Trim cheese slices to size of tomato slices.

3. Place tomato and cheese slices in large, shallow bowl or glass baking dish. Pour dressing over slices. Marinate, covered, in refrigerator for at least 30 minutes or up to 3 hours, turning slices occasionally.

4. Layer basil leaves with largest leaf on bottom, then roll up jelly-roll fashion. Slice basil roll into ¼-inch-thick slices; separate into strips.

5. Arrange tomato and cheese slices alternately on serving plate or 4 individual salad plates. Sprinkle with basil strips; drizzle with remaining dressing.

Makes 4 servings

Step 2. Trimming cheese slices to size of tomato slices.

Step 3. Pouring dressing over cheese and tomato slices for marinating.

Step 4. Slicing basil into strips.

Fennel, Olive and Radicchio Salad

11 Italian- or Greek-style black olives, divided
¹/₄ cup olive oil
1 tablespoon lemon juice
1 flat anchovy fillet *or*
    ¹/₂ teaspoon anchovy paste
¹/₄ teaspoon salt
    Generous dash freshly ground black pepper
    Generous dash sugar
1 fresh fennel bulb
1 head radicchio*
    Fennel greenery for garnish

*Radicchio, a tart red chicory, is available in large supermarkets and specialty food shops. If not available, 2 heads of Belgian endive can be used; although it does not provide the dramatic red color, it will give a similar texture and its slightly bitter flavor will go well with the robust dressing and the sweet anise flavor of fennel.

1. For dressing, cut 3 olives in half; remove and discard pits (technique on page 44). Place pitted olives, oil, lemon juice and anchovy in food processor or blender; process 5 seconds. Add salt, pepper and sugar; process until olives are finely chopped, about 5 seconds more. Set aside.

2. Cut off and discard fennel stalks. Cut off and discard root end at base of fennel bulb and any discolored parts of bulb. Cut fennel bulb lengthwise into 8 wedges; separate each wedge into segments.

3. Separate radicchio leaves; rinse thoroughly under running water. Drain well.

4. Arrange radicchio leaves, fennel and remaining olives on serving plate. Spoon dressing over salad. Garnish, if desired. Serve immediately. *Makes 4 servings*

Step 1. Processing dressing.

Step 2. Cutting fennel bulb.

Step 3. Cleaning radicchio leaves.

Marinated Vegetable Salad

3½ tablespoons white wine vinegar
2 tablespoons minced fresh basil
or ½ teaspoon dried basil
leaves, crushed
½ teaspoon salt
⅛ teaspoon pepper
Dash sugar
6 tablespoons olive oil
2 ripe medium tomatoes
⅓ cup pitted green olives
⅓ cup Italian- or Greek-style
black olives
1 head leaf or red leaf lettuce
1 small head curly endive
2 heads Belgian endive

1. For dressing, place vinegar, basil, salt, pepper and sugar in food processor or blender. With motor running, add oil in slow steady stream until oil is thoroughly blended.

2. Cut tomatoes into quarters. Combine tomatoes and green and black olives in medium bowl. Add dressing; toss lightly. Cover and let stand at room temperature 30 minutes to blend flavors, stirring occasionally.

3. Rinse leaf lettuce and curly endive; drain well. Refrigerate greens until ready to assemble salad. Core Belgian endive and separate leaves; rinse and drain well.

4. To serve, layer leaf lettuce, curly endive and Belgian endive leaves in large, shallow serving bowl.

5. Remove tomatoes and olives with slotted spoon and place on top of greens. Spoon remaining dressing over salad. Serve immediately or cover and refrigerate up to 30 minutes.   *Makes 6 servings*

Step 1. Adding oil through feed tube while processing.

Step 3. Coring Belgian endive.

Step 4. Layering leaves in serving bowl.

Fried Eggplant

1 medium eggplant
    (about 1 pound)
1 teaspoon salt
6 ounces mozzarella cheese
½ teaspoon active dry yeast
1½ cups warm water
    (105°F to 115°F)
2 cups all-purpose flour, divided
⅛ teaspoon pepper
4½ tablespoons olive oil, divided
2 tablespoons minced fresh basil
    or ½ teaspoon dried basil
    leaves, crushed
    Vegetable oil
1 egg white
    Lemon slices (optional)
    Fresh basil leaf for garnish

1. Rinse eggplant; cut crosswise into ¼-inch-thick slices. Place in large colander over bowl; sprinkle with salt. Drain 1 hour.

2. Cut cheese into ⅛-inch-thick slices. Trim cheese slices to size of eggplant slices. Wrap in plastic; set aside.

3. Sprinkle yeast over warm water in medium bowl; stir until dissolved. Whisk in 1½ cups flour and pepper until smooth. Let batter stand at room temperature 30 minutes.

4. Rinse eggplant and drain well; pat slices dry between paper towels. Heat 1½ tablespoons olive oil in large skillet over medium-high heat; add as many eggplant slices in single layer without crowding to hot oil. Cook 2 minutes per side until slices are light brown. Remove with slotted spatula; drain on paper towels. Repeat with remaining olive oil and eggplant slices.

5. Sprinkle cheese slices with basil. Place each cheese slice between 2 eggplant slices; press firmly together. Spread remaining ½ cup flour on plate. Dip eggplant stacks in flour to coat lightly.

6. Heat 1½ inches vegetable oil in large saucepan to 350°F. Adjust heat to maintain temperature. Beat egg white in small bowl with electric mixer at high speed until stiff peaks form; fold into yeast batter. Dip eggplant stacks, 1 at a time, into batter; gently shake off excess. Fry stacks in oil, 3 at a time, 2 minutes per side until browned. Remove with slotted spatula; drain on paper towels. Serve hot with lemon slices. Garnish, if desired. *Makes 4 to 6 servings*

Step 1. Slicing eggplant.

Step 5. Placing cheese slices between eggplant slices.

Step 6. Frying eggplant stacks.

Spinach Gnocchi

2 packages (10 ounces) frozen
    chopped spinach
1 cup ricotta cheese
2 eggs
²/₃ cup freshly grated Parmesan
    cheese (about 2 ounces),
    divided
1 cup *plus* 3 tablespoons
    all-purpose flour, divided
¹/₂ teaspoon salt
¹/₈ teaspoon pepper
¹/₈ teaspoon nutmeg
3 tablespoons butter or
    margarine, melted

1. Cook spinach according to package directions. Drain well; let cool. Squeeze spinach dry; place in medium bowl. Stir in ricotta cheese. Add eggs; mix well. Add ¹/₃ cup Parmesan cheese, 3 tablespoons flour, salt, pepper and nutmeg; mix well. Cover and refrigerate 1 hour.

2. Spread remaining 1 cup flour in shallow baking pan. Press a heaping tablespoonful of spinach mixture between a spoon and your hand to form oval gnocchi; place on flour. Repeat with remaining spinach mixture.

3. Roll gnocchi lightly in flour to coat evenly; discard excess flour. Drop 8 to 12 gnocchi into large pot of boiling salted water; reduce heat to medium.

4. Cook, uncovered, 5 minutes or until gnocchi are slightly puffed and slightly firm to the touch. Remove gnocchi with slotted spoon; drain on paper towels. Immediately transfer to greased *broilerproof* shallow baking dish. Reheat water to boiling. Repeat with remaining gnocchi in batches of 8 to 12. Arrange gnocchi in single layer in baking dish.

5. Preheat broiler. Spoon butter over gnocchi; sprinkle with remaining ¹/₃ cup cheese. Broil gnocchi 5 inches from heat source 2 to 3 minutes until cheese melts and browns lightly. Serve immediately. Garnish as desired.

Makes 4 to 6 servings (about 24 gnocchi)

Step 2. Shaping gnocchi.

Step 3. Boiling flour-coated gnocchi.

Step 4. Removing gnocchi with slotted spoon to paper towels.

Risotto alla Milanese

¼ teaspoon saffron threads
3½ to 4 cups chicken broth, divided
7 tablespoons butter or
    margarine, divided
1 large onion, chopped
1½ cups uncooked Arborio or
    short-grain white rice
½ cup dry white wine
½ teaspoon salt
    Dash pepper
¼ cup freshly grated Parmesan
    cheese
    Chopped fresh parsley, fresh
    parsley sprig and tomato
    slices for garnish

1. Crush saffron in mortar with pestle to a powder.

2. Bring broth to a boil in small saucepan over medium heat; reduce heat to low. Stir ½ cup broth into saffron to dissolve; set aside. Keep remaining broth hot.

3. Heat 6 tablespoons butter in large, heavy skillet or 2½-quart saucepan over medium heat until melted and bubbly. Cook and stir onion in hot butter 5 minutes or until onion is soft. Stir in rice; cook and stir 2 minutes. Stir in wine, salt and pepper. Cook, uncovered, over medium-high heat 3 to 5 minutes until wine has evaporated, stirring occasionally.

4. Measure ½ cup hot broth; stir into rice. Reduce heat to medium-low, maintaining a simmer throughout steps 4 and 5. Cook and stir until broth has absorbed. Repeat, adding ½ cup broth 3 more times, cooking and stirring until broth has absorbed.

5. Add saffron-flavored broth to rice and cook until absorbed. Continue adding remaining broth, ½ cup at a time, and cooking until rice is tender but firm and mixture has slightly creamy consistency. (Not all the broth may be necessary. Total cooking time of rice will be about 20 minutes.)

6. Remove risotto from heat. Stir in remaining 1 tablespoon butter and cheese. Garnish, if desired. Serve immediately.

Makes 6 to 8 servings

Step 1. Crushing saffron threads.

Step 3. Stirring rice into onion mixture.

Step 4. Stirring broth into rice until absorbed.

Classic Polenta

6 cups water
2 teaspoons salt
2 cups yellow cornmeal
¼ cup vegetable oil

1. Bring water and salt to a boil in large, heavy saucepan over medium-high heat. Stirring water vigorously, add cornmeal in very thin but steady stream (do not let lumps form). Reduce heat to low.

2. Cook polenta, uncovered, 40 to 60 minutes until very thick, stirring frequently. Polenta is ready when spoon will stand upright by itself in center of mixture. Polenta can be served at this point.*

3. For fried polenta, spray 11 × 7-inch baking pan with nonstick cooking spray. Spread polenta mixture evenly into baking pan. Cover and let stand at room temperature at least 6 hours or until completely cooled and firm.

4. Unmold polenta onto cutting board. Cut polenta crosswise into 1¼-inch-wide strips. Cut strips into 2- to 3-inch-long pieces.

5. Heat oil in large, heavy skillet over medium-high heat; reduce heat to medium. Fry polenta pieces, ½ at a time, 4 to 5 minutes until golden on all sides, turning as needed. Garnish as desired. *Makes 6 to 8 servings*

*Polenta is an important component of Northern Italian cooking. The basic preparation presented here can be served in two forms. Hot freshly made polenta, prepared through step 2, can be mixed with ⅓ cup butter and ⅓ cup grated Parmesan cheese and served as a first course. Or, pour onto a large platter and top with Bolognese Sauce (page 22) or your favorite spaghetti sauce for a main dish. Fried polenta, as prepared here, is appropriate as an appetizer or as a side dish with meat.

Step 1. Stirring cornmeal into boiling water.

Step 3. Spreading polenta into baking pan.

Step 5. Frying polenta.

Tiramisu

1 recipe Zabaglione (page 72)
²/₃ cup heavy or whipping cream, chilled
4 tablespoons sugar, divided
1 pound mascarpone cheese* (about 2¹/₄ cups)
¹/₃ cup freshly brewed espresso or strong coffee
¹/₄ cup Cognac or brandy
1 tablespoon vanilla extract
3 packages (3 ounces each) ladyfingers, split
3 ounces bittersweet or semisweet chocolate, grated
1 tablespoon cocoa powder
  Edible flowers, such as pansies, for garnish**

*Mascarpone is available at Italian markets and some specialty stores. If unavailable, blend 2 packages (8 ounces each) softened cream cheese with ¹/₂ cup heavy or whipping cream and 5 tablespoons sour cream.

**Be sure to use only non-toxic flowers.

1. Prepare Zabaglione. Cover and refrigerate until well chilled.

2. Beat cream with 2 tablespoons sugar in large bowl until soft peaks form. Gently fold in mascarpone cheese, then Zabaglione. (If Zabaglione has separated, beat until well mixed before folding into mascarpone.) Refrigerate 3 hours or until well chilled.

3. Combine espresso, cognac, remaining 2 tablespoons sugar and vanilla extract.

4. Layer ¹/₄ of ladyfingers in flower-petal design in 2-quart glass bowl with straight sides or trifle dish.

5. Generously brush ladyfingers with espresso mixture. Spoon ¹/₄ of cheese mixture over ladyfingers to within 1 inch of side of bowl. Sprinkle with ¹/₄ of grated chocolate.

6. Repeat layers 3 more times using remaining ladyfingers, espresso mixture and grated chocolate. (For garnish, sprinkle remaining ¹/₄ of grated chocolate around edge of dessert, if desired.)

continued on page 72

Step 2. Folding Zabaglione into whipped cream mixture.

Step 4. Layering ladyfingers.

Step 5. Brushing ladyfingers with espresso mixture.

Tiramisu, continued

7. Sift cocoa powder over top with small sieve or tea strainer. Cover and refrigerate at least 30 minutes or until chilled. Garnish, if desired.

Makes 8 to 10 servings

Zabaglione

5 egg yolks
¹/₄ cup sugar
¹/₂ cup marsala, divided
¹/₄ cup dry white wine

1. Place egg yolks in top of double boiler; add sugar. Beat with portable electric mixer at medium speed or rotary beater until mixture is pale yellow and creamy.

2. Place water in bottom of double boiler. Bring to a boil over high heat; reduce heat to low. Place top of double boiler over simmering water. Gradually beat ¹/₄ cup marsala into egg yolk mixture. Beat 1 minute. Gradually beat in remaining ¹/₄ cup marsala and white wine.

3. Continue cooking custard over gently simmering water 6 to 10 minutes until mixture is fluffy and thick enough to form soft mounds when dropped from beaters, beating constantly and scraping bottom and sides of pan frequently. (Watch carefully and *do not overcook* or custard will curdle.) Immediately remove top of double boiler from water. Whisk custard briefly.***

***Zabaglione can be served as its own recipe. Pour into 4 individual serving dishes. Serve immediately with fresh berries and/or cookies.

Makes 4 servings

Step 7. Sifting cocoa powder over Tiramisu.

Zabaglione: Step 2. Adding marsala to egg yolk mixture.

Zabaglione: Step 3. Beating custard until soft mounds form.

Cannoli Pastries

18 to 20 Cannoli Pastry Shells
(recipe follows)
2 pounds ricotta cheese
1½ cups sifted powdered sugar
2 teaspoons ground cinnamon
¼ cup diced candied orange peel,
minced
1 teaspoon grated lemon peel
Powdered sugar
2 ounces semisweet chocolate,
finely chopped
Orange peel strips and fresh
mint leaves for garnish

1. Prepare Cannoli Pastry Shells; set aside.

2. For cannoli filling, beat cheese in large bowl with electric mixer at medium speed until smooth. Add 1½ cups powdered sugar and cinnamon; beat at high speed 3 minutes. Add candied orange peel and lemon peel to cheese mixture; mix well. Cover and refrigerate until ready to serve.

3. To assemble, spoon cheese filling into pastry bag fitted with large plain tip. Pipe about ¼ cup filling into each reserved cannoli pastry shell.*

4. Roll Cannoli Pastries in additional powdered sugar to coat. Dip ends of pastries into chocolate. Arrange pastries on serving plate. Garnish, if desired.

Makes 18 to 20 pastries

*Do not fill Cannoli Pastry Shells ahead of time or shells will become soggy.

Step 3. Piping cheese filling into cannoli pastry shells.

Cannoli Pastry Shells: Step 1. Cutting butter into flour mixture.

Cannoli Pastry Shells

1¾ cups all-purpose flour
2 tablespoons granulated sugar
1 teaspoon grated lemon peel
2 tablespoons butter or margarine, cold
1 egg
6 tablespoons marsala
Vegetable oil

1. Mix flour, granulated sugar and lemon peel in medium bowl; cut in butter with pastry blender or 2 knives until mixture resembles fine crumbs.

continued on page 74

Cannoli Pastries, continued

2. Beat egg and marsala in small bowl; add to flour mixture. Stir with fork to form ball. Divide dough in half; shape into two 1-inch-thick square pieces. Wrap in plastic wrap and refrigerate at least 1 hour.

3. Heat 1½ inches oil in large saucepan to 325°F.

4. Working with 1 piece of dough at a time, roll out on lightly floured surface to ¹⁄₁₆-inch thickness. Cut dough with knife into 9 or 10 (3 × 4-inch) rectangles.

5. Wrap each rectangle around a greased metal cannoli form or an uncooked cannelloni pasta shell. Brush one edge of rectangle lightly with water; overlap with other edge and press firmly to seal.

6. Fry 2 or 3 cannoli pastry shells at a time, 1 to 1½ minutes until light brown, turning once. Remove with tongs; drain on paper towels.

7. Cool until easy to handle. Carefully remove fried pastries from cannoli forms or pasta shells; cool completely. Repeat with remaining piece of dough.

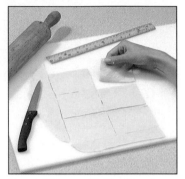

Cannoli Pastry Shells: Step 4. Cutting dough into rectangles.

Cannoli Pastry Shells: Step 5. Wrapping dough around cannelloni shell.

Cannoli Pastry Shells: Step 6. Removing shells to paper towels.

Classic Anise Biscotti

4 ounces whole blanched almonds
(about ³/₄ cup)
2¹/₄ cups all-purpose flour
1 teaspoon baking powder
³/₄ teaspoon salt
³/₄ cup sugar
¹/₂ cup unsalted butter, softened
3 eggs
2 tablespoons brandy
2 teaspoons grated lemon peel
1 tablespoon whole anise seeds

1. Preheat oven to 375°F. To toast almonds, spread almonds on baking sheet. Bake 6 to 8 minutes until toasted and light brown. Remove almonds with spoon to cutting board; cool. Coarsely chop almonds.

2. Combine flour, baking powder and salt in small bowl. Beat sugar and butter in medium bowl with electric mixer at medium speed until light and fluffy. Add eggs, 1 at a time, beating well after each addition and scraping sides of bowl often. Stir in brandy and lemon peel. Add flour mixture gradually; stir until smooth. Stir in almonds and anise seeds. Cover and refrigerate dough 1 hour or until firm.

3. Preheat oven to 375°F. Grease large baking sheet. Divide dough in half. Shape ¹/₂ of dough into 12×2-inch log on lightly floured surface. (Dough will be fairly soft.) Pat smooth with lightly floured fingertips. Repeat with remaining ¹/₂ of dough to form second log.

4. Bake 20 to 25 minutes until logs are light golden brown. Remove baking sheet from oven to wire rack; turn off oven. Cool logs completely.

5. Preheat oven to 350°F. Cut logs diagonally with serrated knife into ¹/₂-inch-thick slices. Place slices flat in single layer on 2 ungreased baking sheets.

6. Bake 8 minutes. Turn slices over; bake 10 to 12 minutes more until cut surfaces are light brown and cookies are dry. Remove cookies to wire racks; cool completely. Store cookies in airtight container up to 2 weeks.

Makes about 4 dozen cookies

Step 1. Chopping almonds.

Step 3. Shaping dough into logs.

Step 5. Slicing baked logs.

Italian Ice

1 cup fruity white wine
1 cup water
1 cup sugar
1 cup lemon juice
2 egg whites*
 Fresh berries (optional)
 Mint leaves for garnish

*Use eggs with clean, uncracked shells.

1. Place wine and water in small saucepan; add sugar. Cook over medium-high heat until sugar has dissolved and syrup boils, stirring frequently. Cover; boil 1 minute. Uncover; adjust heat to maintain simmer. Simmer 10 minutes without stirring. Remove from heat. Refrigerate 1 hour or until syrup is completely cool.

2. Stir lemon juice into cooled syrup. Pour into 9-inch round cake pan. Freeze 1 hour.

3. Quickly stir mixture with fork breaking up ice crystals. Freeze 1 hour more or until firm but not solid. Meanwhile, place medium bowl in freezer to chill.

4. Beat egg whites in small bowl with electric mixer at high speed until stiff peaks form. Remove lemon ice mixture from cake pan to chilled bowl. Immediately beat ice with whisk or fork until smooth. Fold in egg whites; mix well. Spread egg mixture evenly into same cake pan.

5. Freeze 30 minutes. Immediately stir with fork; cover cake pan with foil. Freeze at least 3 hours or until firm.

6. To serve, scoop Italian Ice into fluted champagne glasses or dessert dishes. Serve with berries. Garnish with mint leaves.

Makes 4 servings

Step 2. Pouring cooled syrup into cake pan.

Step 3. Breaking up ice crystals.

Step 4. Folding beaten egg whites into frozen mixture.

STEP-BY-STEP COOKING

MEXICAN

Baked Shrimp with Chili-Garlic Butter *(page 136)*

CLASS NOTES

Tacos, burritos, enchiladas—once considered exotic foods, they are now as familiar as earlier imports of pizza, quiche and egg rolls. Due to their vibrant flavors, enticing textural contrasts and eye-catching colors, these Mexican dishes have been readily accepted into our menus.

Mexican cuisine is more diverse than the taco lover might suspect. Based on foods such as corn, tomatoes, chilies and beans, this cuisine has developed over centuries and was shaped by unique geography, climate, indigenous foods and the native Indian culture. Mexican cuisine was also enhanced, but not overshadowed, by the Spanish introduction of their cooking techniques and domestic animals.

The recipes in this book were chosen to illustrate the variety of this wonderful cuisine; they range from subtle to spicy, simple to complex, rustic to sophisticated. Using authentic ingredients and cooking techniques, and presented with clear instructions and how-to photos, these dishes are sure to be a success even for the novice cook.

EQUIPMENT

Mexican cuisine requires very little in the way of specialized equipment, but a few items call for some discussion.

Bean Masher: A solid wooden block or perforated metal disk attached to a handle, this tool is very useful for the proper stirring and mashing needed to make refried beans. If necessary, a potato masher can be substituted.

Mortar and Pestle: Used to grind whole spices, herbs and nuts into a powder. The mortar is a bowl-shaped container and the pestle is a rounded-bottomed utensil. The mortar and pestle come as a set and are made out of marble, hardwood, porcelain or stoneware.

Spice or Coffee Grinder, Electric: A small appliance that effectively and quickly grinds whole spices. It can be used to prepare pure fresh chili powder from whole dried chilies. It is also used to grind seeds and nuts into the fine powder that is needed for some sauces, a function neither the blender nor food processor performs as well.

Tortilla Press: The press consists of two flat metal disks (usually 6 inches in diameter) that are hinged on one side and have a pressing handle attached at the opposite side. It is inexpensive and readily available in cookware shops and Mexican markets. A tortilla press is essential for speed and accuracy if you plan to make corn tortillas on a regular basis. However, you can improvise pressing the dough with the bottom of a heavy skillet or pie plate.

MEXICAN INGREDIENTS

These ingredients are normally available in Mexican groceries. Many can be found in supermarkets and gourmet food stores and some can be purchased in other Latin American, Caribbean and even Oriental food stores.

Annatto Seeds (also called achiote): Small, hard crimson-colored seeds used primarily in the Mayan-based cooking of the Yucatan. The seeds impart a deep yellow color and mild but distinctive flavor. They are soaked to soften or ground to a fine powder before using.

Chayote: A pear-shaped, pale green, soft-skinned squash with a delicious delicate flavor. It is also called mirliton or christophene. Chayote is generally available in the winter months and can be eaten raw, sautéed or baked. Store it in a plastic bag in the refrigerator for up to one month.

Chilies: See the descriptions on pages 84–85.

Chorizo: An orange- or red-colored, coarse-textured pork sausage sold bulk-style or stuffed into casings. The flavor ranges from highly seasoned to quite hot. Always remove the casing before using.

Cilantro (also called fresh coriander or Chinese parsley): A pungent herb with green delicate leaves, similar in appearance, but not flavor, to flat-leaf parsley. Used extensively in Mexican cooking, there is no substitute. Store it in the refrigerator for up to one week with the stems in a glass of water; cover the leaves with a plastic bag.

Jícama: A root vegetable with thin tan-brown skin and crisp, sweetish, white flesh. Shaped like a large turnip, jícama is most often used raw in salads or eaten as a refreshing snack. It should be peeled before using. Store it in the refrigerator for up to five days.

Masa Harina: A specially prepared flour used to make corn tortillas, tamales and other corn-based doughs. It is commonly available in 5-pound bags.

Mexican Chocolate: A mixture of chocolate, almonds, sugar and sometimes cinnamon and vanilla, ground together and formed into octagonal tablets. It is used in desserts, frothy chocolate beverages and, in small amounts, to add a subtle flavor enrichment to some mole sauces.

Onions: White onions with a sharp bite are used in Mexican cooking and are necessary for flavor balance and authenticity. Yellow onions are too mild and impart an undesirable sweetness when cooked.

Queso Chihuahua: A rich semi-soft cheese with a creamy color, mild flavor and good melting qualities. Mild Cheddar, Monterey Jack or Muenster can be used as substitutes.

Tomatillo (also called tomate verde or Mexican tomato): A small hard, green fruit with a papery outer husk that is pulled off before using. Tomatillos have a distinct acidic flavor and are used extensively in cooked sauces. They are available fresh or canned (often labeled tomatillo entero). There is no substitute.

Tortillas: The mainstay of Mexican cuisine. These thin, flat breads are made of corn or wheat flour. Nothing can compare with the taste and texture of freshly made tortillas, but making them at home (see recipes on pages 153 and 154) requires some practice and skill. Tortillas are readily available in the supermarket and these may be substituted for homemade tortillas. Corn tortillas usually measure between 5 and 6 inches in diameter; flour tortillas are available in many sizes, ranging from 7 to 12 inches in diameter.

CHILIES

The subject of chilies can be very confusing for beginning and experienced cooks alike. There are over 100 varieties of chilies in Mexico, each with its own unique characteristics. They are used both fresh and dried and either type can be whole or ground. The same chili can even be found under different names depending upon its region of origin. Chilies range in degree of heat from very mild to incendiary, and the heat can vary within a variety.

Due to increasing interest in Mexican foods, chilies that were once available only in Mexican grocery stores are now readily available in gourmet food stores and many local supermarkets. However, not all chilies will be available in all areas at all times. The following descriptions of the more common varieties will provide you with a basic knowledge of individual chili traits. With this knowledge, you can substitute one chili for another with similar traits. The character of the dish may change slightly, but it will still be delicious and enjoyable.

A Note of Caution: The heat of chilies comes from the seeds, the veins (the thin inner membranes to which the seeds are attached) and in the parts nearest the veins. For milder dishes, the veins and seeds are removed and discarded. The oils from the seeds and veins can be very irritating to the skin and can cause painful burning of the hands, eyes and lips. Do not touch your face while handling chilies and wash your hands well in warm soapy water after handling. Wear rubber gloves if your skin is especially sensitive or if you are handling a number of chilies.

Fresh Chilies

Fresh chilies will keep for several weeks refrigerated in a plastic bag lined with paper towels. (The towels absorb any moisture.) When purchasing fresh chilies, select those that have firm, unblemished skin.

From left to right: Anaheim, Jalapeño, Poblano and Serrano chilies

Anaheim (also called California green chili): A light green chili that has a mild flavor with a slight bite. They are 4 to 6 inches long, about 1½ inches wide and have a rounded tip. Anaheims are also sold canned. For a spicier flavor, poblano chilies can be substituted.

Jalapeño: A small, dark green chili, normally 2 to 3 inches long and about ¾ inch wide with a blunt or slightly tapered end. Their flavor varies from hot to very hot. They are also sold canned and pickled. Serranos or any other small, hot, fresh chilies can be substituted.

Poblano: A very dark green, large triangular-shaped chili with a pointed end. Poblanos are usually 3½ to 5 inches long. Their flavor ranges from mild to quite hot. For a milder flavor, Anaheims can be substituted.

Serrano: A medium green, very small chili with a very hot flavor. It usually ranges from 1 to 1½ inches

in length and is about ⅜ inch wide with a pointed end. Serranos are also available pickled. Jalapeños or any other small, hot, fresh chilies can be substituted.

Dried Chilies

Dried red (ripe) chilies are usually sold in cellophane packages of various weights. They will keep indefinitely if stored in a tightly covered container in a cool, dark, dry place.

From left to right: Pasilla, Pequín, Mulato, De árbol and Ancho chilies

Ancho: A fairly large, triangular-shaped chili, slightly smaller than the mulato chili. It has wrinkled, medium to dark reddish-brown skin. Anchos are full-flavored, ranging from mild to medium-hot.

Chipotle: A smoked and dried jalapeño chili. It has wrinkled, medium-brown skin and a rich, smoky, very hot flavor. Chipotles are also commonly available canned in adobo sauce.

De árbol: A very small, slender, almost needle-shaped chili with

smooth, bright red skin and a very hot flavor.

Mulato: A triangular-shaped, large chili that has wrinkled, blackish-brown skin. Its flavor is rich, pungent and medium-hot.

Pasilla: A long, slender, medium-sized chili with wrinkled, blackish-brown skin. It has a pungent flavor, ranging from mild to quite hot. (Pasillas are sometimes labeled "negro chilies.")

Pequín (also spelled piquín): A very tiny chili shaped like an oval bead. It has a slightly wrinkled, orangish-red skin. Use pequín chilies with caution as their flavor is very, very hot. (These are sometimes labeled "tepin chilies.")

HELPFUL PREPARATION TECHNIQUES

Roasting Fresh Chilies: Using tongs to hold the chili, place it directly in the medium flame of a gas burner; roast, turning as needed, until the chili is evenly blistered and charred.

Immediately place the roasted chili into a plastic bag; close the

bag. Repeat with the remaining chilies. To roast in the broiler, place the chilies on a foil-lined broiler rack; roast them 2 to 3 inches from the heat until they are evenly blistered and charred, turning as needed. Place the roasted chilies in a plastic bag; close the bag.

Let the roasted chilies stand in the closed plastic bag 20 minutes. Peel each chili under cold running water, rubbing and pulling off the

charred skin. Slit the chili open lengthwise using scissors or a knife. Carefully pull out and discard the seeds and veins. Rinse the chilies well and drain; pat them dry with paper towels.

Toasting Dried Chilies: Heat an ungreased griddle or heavy skillet over medium heat; place the chilies on the griddle in a single layer. Cook the chilies 1 to 3 minutes until the color changes slightly (*but do not burn*) and the chilies become fragrant (*but not to the point of emitting a harsh aroma*), pressing them down with a spatula and turning over occasionally. If you are toasting a large number of dried chilies, place them in a single layer on a baking sheet in a 350°F oven 3 to 5 minutes until the chilies are hot to the touch and fragrant. When the chilies are cool enough to handle but still pliable, cut each one

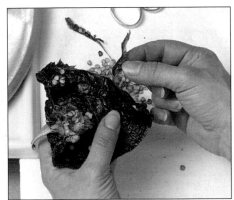

open lengthwise with scissors; carefully pull out the seeds and the veins. Only if the recipe specifies, rinse and rub chilies under cold running water.

Broiling Tomatoes: Place whole tomatoes on a foil-lined broiler rack. Broil the tomatoes 4 inches from the heat 15 to 20 minutes until the tomatoes are evenly blistered and dark brown (*not black*) on outside and soft throughout, turning as needed. Use the entire tomato; do not skin, seed or core.

Softening and Warming Tortillas: Stack the tortillas and wrap in foil. Heat the tortillas in a 350°F oven 10 minutes until the tortillas are warm. Or, warm them in a microwave oven. Stack the tortillas and wrap them in plastic wrap; microwave on HIGH ½ to 1 minute, turning them over and rotating ¼ turn once during heating.

Cheesy Chorizo Wedges

Red & Green Salsa (recipe follows) (optional)
8 ounces chorizo
1 cup (4 ounces) shredded mild Cheddar cheese
1 cup (4 ounces) shredded Monterey Jack cheese
3 flour tortillas (10-inch diameter)

1. Prepare Red & Green Salsa.

2. Remove and discard casing from chorizo. Heat medium skillet over high heat until hot. Reduce heat to medium. Crumble chorizo into skillet. Brown 6 to 8 minutes, stirring to separate meat. Remove with slotted spoon; drain on paper towels.

3. Preheat oven to 450°F. Mix cheeses in bowl.

4. Place tortillas on baking sheets. Divide chorizo evenly among tortillas, leaving ½ inch of edges of tortillas uncovered. Sprinkle cheese mixture over top.

5. Bake 8 to 10 minutes until edges are crisp and golden and cheese is bubbly and melted.

6. Transfer to serving plates; cut each tortilla into 6 wedges. Sprinkle Red & Green Salsa on wedges, if desired. *Makes 6 to 8 servings*

Red & Green Salsa

1 small red bell pepper
¼ cup coarsely chopped cilantro
3 green onions, cut into thin slices
2 fresh jalapeño chilies, seeded, minced
2 tablespoons fresh lime juice
1 clove garlic, minced
¼ teaspoon salt

Cut bell pepper lengthwise in half; remove and discard seeds and veins. Cut halves lengthwise into thin slivers; cut slivers crosswise into halves. Mix all ingredients in bowl. Let stand, covered, at room temperature 1 to 2 hours to blend flavors. *Makes 1 cup*

Step 2. Removing casing from chorizo.

Step 2. Browning chorizo.

Step 4. Sprinkling cheese mixture over tortilla.

Nachos Olé

1½ cups Refried Beans (page 152)
or canned refried beans
6 dozen Corn Tortilla Chips
(page 155) or packaged corn
tortilla chips
1½ cups (6 ounces) shredded
Monterey Jack cheese
1½ cups (6 ounces) shredded
Cheddar cheese
1 large tomato
½ cup thinly sliced pickled
jalapeño chilies

1. Prepare Refried Beans.

2. Prepare Corn Tortilla Chips.

3. Preheat oven to 400°F. Combine cheeses in small bowl. Reheat beans, if necessary.

4. Cut tomato crosswise in half. Gently squeeze each half to remove and discard seeds. Chop tomato.

5. Spread 1 teaspoon beans on each tortilla chip.

6. Arrange chips in single layer with edges overlapping slightly on 2 to 3 baking sheets or large ovenproof plates.

7. Sprinkle chips evenly with tomato and chilies; sprinkle with cheese mixture.

8. Bake 5 to 8 minutes until cheese is bubbly and melted.   *Makes 4 to 6 servings*

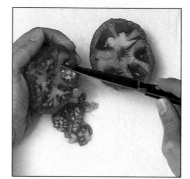

Step 4. Gently squeezing tomato half to remove seeds.

Step 5. Spreading beans on tortilla chips.

Step 7. Sprinkling chips with cheese mixture.

Cheese & Chorizo Burritos

Onion-Chili Relish* (recipe follows)
24 corn tortillas (4-inch diameter) *or* 6 flour tortillas (8-inch diameter), cut into quarters
8 ounces queso Chihuahua or Monterey Jack cheese
4 to 6 ounces chorizo
Chilies for garnish

*Or, substitute Fresh Tomato Salsa (page 106) for the Onion-Chili Relish.

1. Prepare Onion-Chili Relish.

2. Preheat oven to 400°F. Wrap tortillas in foil.

3. Cut cheese into very thin slices. Divide slices evenly among 4 to 6 small, ovenproof plates. (Or, place slices in 1 large, shallow casserole.)

4. Remove and discard casing from chorizo. Heat medium skillet over high heat until hot. Reduce heat to medium. Crumble chorizo into skillet. Brown 6 to 8 minutes; stir to separate meat. Remove with slotted spoon; drain on paper towels. Keep warm.

5. Bake cheese 3 minutes. Place tortillas in oven; continue baking 4 minutes more or until cheese is melted.

6. Place tortillas in serving bowl; sprinkle chorizo evenly over cheese. To serve, spoon cheese mixture onto tortillas and top with relish; fold tortilla around filling. Garnish, if desired.

Makes 4 to 6 servings

Step 3. Cutting cheese into very thin slices.

Step 4. Removing casing from chorizo.

Onion-Chili Relish

1 medium white onion
1 or 2 fresh jalapeño chilies
3 tablespoons fresh lime juice
¼ teaspoon salt

1. Cut onion and chilies lengthwise into halves. Remove and discard seeds from chilies. Cut onion and chili halves lengthwise into very thin slices; separate into slivers.

2. Combine all ingredients in bowl; mix well. Let stand, covered, at room temperature 2 hours to blend flavors. *Makes about 1 cup*

Onion-Chili Relish: Step 1. Cutting onion.

Classic Guacamole

4 tablespoons finely chopped
  white onion, divided
1½ tablespoons coarsely chopped
  cilantro, divided
1 or 2 fresh serrano or jalapeño
  chilies, seeded, finely chopped
¼ teaspoon chopped garlic
  (optional)
2 large, soft-ripe avocados
1 medium, very ripe tomato
  Boiling water
1 to 2 teaspoons fresh lime juice
¼ teaspoon salt
  Corn Tortilla Chips (page 155)
  or packaged corn tortilla
  chips
  Chilies and cilantro sprig for
  garnish

1. Combine 2 tablespoons onion, 1 tablespoon cilantro, chilies and garlic in large mortar. Grind with pestle until almost smooth. (Mixture can be processed in blender, if necessary, but it will become more watery than desired.)

2. Cut avocados lengthwise into halves; remove and discard pits. Scoop avocado flesh out of shells; place in bowl. Add chili mixture. Mash roughly with wooden spoon, bean masher or potato masher, leaving avocado slightly chunky.

3. To loosen skin from tomato, place tomato in small saucepan of boiling water 30 to 45 seconds. Rinse immediately under cold running water. Peel tomato; cut crosswise in half. Gently squeeze each half to remove and discard seeds. Chop tomato.

4. Add tomato, lime juice, salt and remaining 2 tablespoons onion and ½ tablespoon cilantro to avocado mixture; mix well. Serve immediately or cover and refrigerate up to 4 hours. Serve with Corn Tortilla Chips. Garnish, if desired. *Makes about 2 cups*

Step 2. Scooping avocado flesh out of shells.

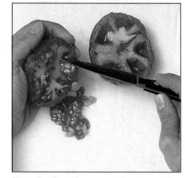

Step 3. Gently squeezing tomato half to remove seeds.

Step 4. Adding tomato to avocado mixture.

Mexican Tortilla Soup

6 to 8 corn tortillas (6-inch diameter), preferably day-old
2 large, very ripe tomatoes, peeled, seeded (about 1 pound) (page 92)
²/₃ cup coarsely chopped white onion
1 large clove garlic
Vegetable oil
7 cups chicken broth
4 sprigs cilantro
3 sprigs fresh mint (optional)
¹/₂ to 1 teaspoon salt
4 or 5 dried pasilla chilies
5 ounces queso Chihuahua or Monterey Jack cheese, cut into ¹/₂-inch cubes
¹/₄ cup coarsely chopped cilantro

1. Stack tortillas; cutting through stack, cut tortillas into ¹/₂-inch-wide strips. Let strips stand, uncovered, on wire rack 1 to 2 hours to dry slightly.

2. Place tomatoes, onion and garlic in blender; process until smooth. Heat 3 tablespoons oil in large saucepan over medium heat until hot. Add tomato mixture. Cook 10 minutes, stirring frequently.

3. Add broth and cilantro sprigs to saucepan; bring to a boil over high heat. Reduce heat to low. Simmer, uncovered, 20 minutes. Add mint and salt; simmer 10 minutes more. Remove and discard cilantro and mint. Keep soup warm.

4. Heat ¹/₂ inch oil in deep, heavy, large skillet over medium-high heat to 375°F; adjust heat to maintain temperature.

5. Fry half of tortilla strips at a time, in single layer, 1 minute or until crisp, turning strips occasionally. Remove with slotted spoon; drain on paper towels.

6. Fry chilies in same oil about 30 seconds or until puffed and crisp, turning chilies occasionally. Do not burn chilies. Drain on paper towels. Cool slightly; crumble coarsely.

7. Ladle soup into bowls. Let each person add chilies, tortilla strips, cheese and chopped cilantro according to taste.

Makes 4 to 6 servings

Step 1. Cutting tortillas into ¹/₂-inch-wide strips.

Step 3. Stirring broth into tomato mixture.

Step 6. Frying chilies.

Gazpacho

6 large, very ripe tomatoes
   (about 3 pounds), divided
1½ cups tomato juice
   1 small clove garlic
   2 tablespoons fresh lime juice
   2 tablespoons olive oil
   1 tablespoon white wine vinegar
   1 teaspoon sugar
   ½ to 1 teaspoon salt
   ½ teaspoon dried oregano leaves,
      crushed
   6 green onions, cut into thin slices
   ¼ cup finely chopped celery
   ¼ cup finely chopped, seeded,
      unpared cucumber
1 or 2 fresh jalapeño chilies,
      seeded, minced
   Garlic Croutons (recipe
      follows) or packaged croutons
   1 cup diced avocado
   1 red or green bell pepper, seeded,
      chopped
   2 tablespoons cilantro
      Lime wedges (optional)
      Sour cream (optional)

1. Seed and finely chop 1 tomato (technique on page 88). Set aside.

2. Coarsely chop remaining 5 tomatoes; process half of tomatoes, ¾ cup tomato juice and garlic in blender until smooth. Press through sieve into large bowl; discard seeds. Repeat with remaining coarsely chopped tomatoes and ¾ cup tomato juice.

3. Whisk lime juice, oil, vinegar, sugar, salt and oregano into tomato mixture. Stir in finely chopped tomato, onions, celery, cucumber and chilies. Cover; refrigerate at least 4 hours or up to 24 hours.

4. Prepare Garlic Croutons.

5. Stir soup; ladle into chilled bowls. Add croutons, avocado, pepper, cilantro, lime wedges and sour cream according to taste.

Makes 2 servings

Garlic Croutons

   5 slices firm white bread
   2 tablespoons olive oil
   1 clove garlic, minced
   ¼ teaspoon paprika

1. Preheat oven to 300°F. Trim crusts from bread; cut into ½-inch cubes.

2. Heat oil in skillet over medium heat. Stir in garlic and paprika. Add bread; cook and stir 1 minute just until bread is evenly coated with oil.

3. Spread bread on baking sheet. Bake 20 to 25 minutes until crisp and golden. Cool.

Makes about 2 cups

Step 2. Pressing tomatoes through sieve.

Step 3. Whisking lime juice into tomato mixture.

Flautas with Chicken Filling

3 chicken breast halves (about
   1½ pounds)
1 can (4 ounces) diced green
   chilies, drained
½ cup water
⅛ teaspoon salt (optional)
½ teaspoon ground cumin
   Fresh Tomato Salsa (page 106)
1 cup Classic Guacamole
   (page 92) or prepared
   guacamole
12 corn tortillas (6-inch diameter)
   Vegetable oil
4 cups shredded iceberg lettuce
1 cup (4 ounces) shredded
   Monterey Jack cheese
½ cup sour cream
   Tomato wedges and cilantro
   sprigs for garnish

1. Combine chicken, chilies, water, salt and cumin in medium skillet. Bring to a boil over medium-high heat. Reduce heat to low. Cover; simmer 15 to 20 minutes until chicken is tender. Remove chicken; let stand until cool enough to handle. Drain chilies; reserve.

2. Prepare Fresh Tomato Salsa and Classic Guacamole.

3. Remove and discard bones and skin from chicken. With fingers, tear chicken into long, thin shreds. Warm corn tortillas (technique on page 85).

4. For each flauta: Overlap 2 tortillas by about half of each tortilla. Spoon ⅛ of chicken mixture down center. Top with ⅛ of reserved chilies. Roll up as tightly as possible.

5. Preheat oven to 250°F. Heat 1 inch oil in deep, heavy skillet over medium-high heat to 375°F; adjust heat to maintain temperature. Line baking sheet with paper towels.

6. Fry flautas, 1 or 2 at a time, in oil, holding closed with tongs during first 30 seconds to prevent flautas from unrolling. Fry 2 minutes or until crisp and golden on all sides, turning occasionally. Drain on paper towels. Keep warm in oven on prepared baking sheet.

7. To serve, place 2 to 3 flautas on each lettuce-lined plate. Top each serving with some of the cheese, Classic Guacamole and sour cream. Garnish, if desired. Serve with Fresh Tomato Salsa.

Makes 4 to 6 servings

Step 1. Adding water to skillet.

Step 4. Forming flauta.

Step 6. Frying flautas.

Chicken Enchiladas

1 broiler-fryer chicken (about
   3 pounds), cut into 8 pieces
3 fresh poblano chilies, roasted,
   peeled, seeded, deveined, diced
   (pages 84–85)
1 large tomato, peeled, seeded,
   chopped (page 92)
$\frac{1}{2}$ cup finely chopped white onion
1 clove garlic, minced
$\frac{1}{2}$ teaspoon ground cumin
$\frac{1}{4}$ teaspoon salt
$\frac{1}{2}$ cup chicken broth
$1\frac{1}{2}$ cups heavy cream
12 corn tortillas (6-inch diameter)
2 cups (8 ounces) shredded queso
   Chihuahua or Monterey Jack
   cheese
Green onions and slivered red
   bell peppers for garnish
Arroz Rojos (page 142)
   (optional)

1. Place chicken in single layer in 12-inch skillet. Sprinkle with chilies, tomato, white onion, garlic, cumin and salt; add broth. Bring to a boil over medium-high heat. Reduce heat. Cover; simmer 1 hour or until chicken is tender.

2. Remove chicken from skillet with tongs, shaking off vegetable pieces. Let stand until cool enough to handle.

3. Skim and discard fat from skillet. Bring remaining broth mixture to a boil over medium-high heat. Boil 4 to 8 minutes until mixture is reduced to 2 cups. Pour reduced broth mixture into 13 × 9-inch baking dish.

4. Remove and discard skin and bones from chicken. Using fingers, pull chicken into coarse shreds.

5. Preheat oven to 375°F. Heat cream in medium skillet over medium heat to just below boiling; remove from heat.

6. Dip 1 tortilla in cream with tongs a few seconds or until limp. Remove, draining off excess cream. Spread about 3 tablespoons chicken down center of tortilla.

7. Roll up; place on sauce in baking dish. Repeat with remaining tortillas, cream and chicken. Pour any remaining cream over enchiladas.

8. Sprinkle cheese over enchiladas. Bake 25 to 30 minutes until sauce is bubbly and cheese is melted. Garnish, if desired. Serve with Arroz Rojos. *Makes 4 to 6 servings*

Step 1. Adding broth to skillet.

Step 6. Dipping tortilla in cream.

Step 7. Forming enchilada.

Chicken Tostadas

2 cups Refried Beans (page 152)
  or canned refried beans
  Fresh Tomato Salsa (page 106)
  Lime-Cumin Dressing (recipe
  follows)
  Vegetable oil
4 flour tortillas (10-inch
  diameter) *or* 8 corn tortillas
  (6-inch diameter)
3 cups shredded cooked chicken
4 cups shredded iceberg lettuce
1 small carrot, shredded
1 cup (4 ounces) shredded mild
  Cheddar cheese, divided
1 large, firm-ripe avocado, pared,
  pitted, sliced
1/2 cup sour cream

1. Prepare Refried Beans, mashing coarsely.

2. Prepare Fresh Tomato Salsa and Lime-Cumin Dressing.

3. Preheat oven to 250°F. Heat 1 inch oil in deep, heavy, large skillet over medium-high heat to 375°F; adjust heat to maintain temperature. Line baking sheet with paper towels.

Step 4. Frying tortilla.

4. Fry tortillas, 1 at a time, in oil 1 minute or until crisp and light brown, turning once. Drain on paper towels. Keep warm in oven on prepared baking sheet.

5. Reheat beans, if necessary. Combine chicken, lettuce and carrot in large bowl. Add dressing; toss to mix.

6. To serve, place 1 flour or 2 corn tortillas on each plate. Spread beans to within 1/2 inch of edge of each tortilla. Sprinkle 3/4 cup cheese evenly over tostadas. Top with chicken mixture and avocado. Garnish with remaining cheese. Serve with Fresh Tomato Salsa and sour cream.   *Makes 4 servings*

Step 6. Sprinkling cheese over tostada.

Lime-Cumin Dressing

  2 tablespoons fresh lime juice
  1/4 teaspoon grated lime peel
  1/4 teaspoon salt
  1/4 teaspoon ground cumin
  1/4 cup vegetable oil

Combine lime juice, lime peel, salt and cumin in small bowl. Gradually add oil, whisking continuously, until thoroughly blended. Store in refrigerator.   *Makes about 1/3 cup*

Lime-Cumin Dressing: Whisking oil into lime juice mixture.

Beef Chimichangas

Fresh Tomato Salsa (page 106)
6 ounces chorizo
1 pound ground beef
$\frac{1}{2}$ cup finely chopped white onion
1 clove garlic, minced
$\frac{1}{2}$ teaspoon ground cumin
1 can (8 ounces) tomato sauce
$\frac{1}{4}$ cup sliced pitted ripe olives .
12 flour tortillas (8-inch diameter)
1 cup (4 ounces) shredded
    Monterey Jack cheese
    Vegetable oil
1 cup sour cream
    Cilantro sprigs and radishes for
    garnish

1. Prepare Fresh Tomato Salsa.

2. Remove and discard casing from chorizo. Heat large skillet over high heat until hot. Reduce heat to medium. Crumble chorizo into skillet. Brown 6 to 8 minutes, stirring to separate meat.

3. Crumble beef into skillet. Brown over medium-high heat 6 to 8 minutes, stirring to separate meat. Add onion, garlic and cumin; cook and stir 4 minutes or until onion is softened. Spoon off and discard fat.

4. Stir in tomato sauce. Bring to a boil over high heat. Reduce heat to low. Cover and simmer 15 minutes. Uncover skillet; increase heat to medium. Cook and stir 5 minutes or until most of liquid has evaporated and meat is moistly coated with sauce. Stir in olives.

5. If not freshly made, soften and warm tortillas (technique on page 85).

6. Place $\frac{1}{4}$ cup meat mixture on bottom half of 1 tortilla; spread to within $1\frac{1}{2}$ inches of bottom and side edges. Sprinkle with slightly rounded tablespoon cheese.

continued on page 106

Step 2. Removing casing from chorizo.

Step 3. Spooning off and discarding fat from skillet.

Step 4. Cooking meat mixture until most of liquid has evaporated.

Beef Chimichangas, continued

7. To form, fold bottom edge of tortilla up over filling; fold in side edges, then roll up to completely enclose filling. Secure top with wooden toothpick.

8. Repeat steps 6 and 7 with remaining tortillas, meat mixture and cheese to make 11 more chimichangas.

9. Preheat oven to 250°F. Heat 1 inch oil in deep, heavy skillet over medium-high heat to 375°F; adjust heat to maintain temperature. Line baking sheet with paper towels.

10. Fry 2 to 3 chimichangas at a time in oil 2 to 3 minutes until golden on all sides, turning occasionally. Remove with tongs; drain on paper towels. Keep warm in oven on prepared baking sheet.

11. Remove toothpicks before serving. Serve with sour cream and Fresh Tomato Salsa. Garnish, if desired.

Makes 6 servings

Fresh Tomato Salsa

1 medium tomato, finely chopped
$1/4$ cup coarsely chopped cilantro
2 tablespoons finely chopped white onion
1 fresh jalapeño chili, seeded, finely chopped
1 tablespoon fresh lime juice

Combine all ingredients in small bowl; mix well. Let stand, covered, at room temperature 1 to 2 hours to blend flavors.   *Makes about $3/4$ cup*

Step 7. Forming chimichanga.

Step 10. Frying chimichangas.

Beef Enchiladas

Red Chili Sauce (page 108)
1 1/2 pounds lean boneless beef
    chuck
1/2 teaspoon salt
2 tablespoons vegetable oil
1/2 cup finely chopped white onion
3/4 cup beef broth
1/4 cup raisins
1 clove garlic, minced
1/2 teaspoon ground cloves
1/4 teaspoon anise seeds, crushed
12 corn tortillas (6-inch diameter)
1 cup (4 ounces) shredded mild
    Cheddar cheese
3/4 cup sour cream
1/3 cup sliced pitted ripe olives
    Basil sprig and tomato wedge
    for garnish

1. Prepare Red Chili Sauce.

2. Cut meat lengthwise with utility knife into 1-inch strips. Then cut crosswise at 1-inch intervals to form 1-inch cubes.

3. Sprinkle beef with salt. Brown half of beef in hot oil in large skillet over medium-high heat 10 to 12 minutes, turning frequently. Remove with slotted spoon to plate. Repeat with remaining beef.

4. Reduce heat to medium. Add onion; cook and stir 4 minutes or until onion is softened. Return beef to skillet. Stir in broth, raisins, garlic, cloves, anise seeds and 1/4 cup Red Chili Sauce. Bring to a boil over medium-high heat. Reduce heat to low. Cover and simmer 1 1/2 to 2 hours until beef is very tender. Using 2 forks, pull beef into coarse shreds in skillet. Remove from heat.

5. Preheat oven to 375°F. Heat remaining Red Chili Sauce in medium skillet over medium heat until hot; remove from heat.

6. Dip 1 tortilla in sauce with tongs a few seconds or until limp. Remove, draining off excess sauce.

continued on page 108

Step 3. Removing beef from skillet with slotted spoon.

Step 4. Pulling beef into coarse shreds.

Step 6. Dipping tortilla in sauce.

Beef Enchiladas, continued

7. Spread about 3 tablespoons meat filling down center of tortilla. Roll up; place in 13×9-inch baking dish. Repeat with remaining tortillas, sauce and meat filling. Pour remaining sauce over enchiladas.

8. Sprinkle cheese over top. Bake 25 minutes or until bubbly and cheese is melted. To serve, spoon sour cream down center of enchiladas. Sprinkle with olives. Garnish, if desired.

Makes 4 to 6 servings

Red Chili Sauce

3 ounces dried ancho chilies (about 5), toasted, seeded, deveined, rinsed (page 85)
2¹/₂ cups boiling water
2 tablespoons vegetable oil
2 tablespoons tomato paste
1 clove garlic, minced
¹/₂ teaspoon salt
¹/₂ teaspoon dried oregano leaves, crushed
¹/₄ teaspoon ground cumin
¹/₄ teaspoon ground coriander

1. Place chilies in medium bowl; cover with boiling water. Let stand 1 hour.

2. Place chilies along with soaking water in blender; process until smooth.

3. Pour into 2-quart saucepan; whisk in remaining ingredients. Bring to a boil over medium-high heat. Reduce heat to very low. Cover and simmer 10 minutes, stirring occasionally.

Makes about 2¹/₂ cups

Note: Sauce can be refrigerated, covered, up to 3 days or frozen up to 1 month.

Step 7. Forming enchilada.

Red Chili Sauce: Step 1. Covering chilies with boiling water.

Red Chili Sauce: Step 3. Whisking remaining ingredients into chili mixture.

Spicy Beef Tacos

1 pound boneless beef chuck, cut
    into 1-inch cubes
Vegetable oil
1 to 2 teaspoons chili powder
1 clove garlic, minced
$\frac{1}{2}$ teaspoon salt
$\frac{1}{2}$ teaspoon ground cumin
1 can (14$\frac{1}{2}$ ounces) whole peeled
    tomatoes, undrained, chopped
12 corn tortillas
    (6-inch diameter)*
1 cup (4 ounces) shredded mild
    Cheddar cheese
2 to 3 cups shredded iceberg
    lettuce
1 large fresh tomato, seeded,
    chopped (page 88)
Cilantro for garnish

*Or, substitute packaged taco shells for the corn tortillas. Omit steps 4 and 5. Warm taco shells according to package directions.

1. Brown beef in 2 tablespoons hot oil in large skillet over medium-high heat 10 to 12 minutes, turning frequently. Reduce heat to low. Stir in chili powder, garlic, salt and cumin. Cook and stir 30 seconds.

2. Add undrained tomatoes. Bring to a boil over high heat. Reduce heat to low. Cover and simmer 1$\frac{1}{2}$ to 2 hours until beef is very tender.

3. Using 2 forks, pull beef into coarse shreds in skillet. Increase heat to medium. Cook, uncovered, 10 to 15 minutes until most of liquid has evaporated and beef is moistly coated with sauce. Keep warm.

4. Heat 4 to 5 inches of oil in deep fat fryer or deep saucepan over medium-high heat to 375°F; adjust heat to maintain temperature.

5. For taco shells, place 1 tortilla in taco fryer basket;** close gently. Fry tortilla $\frac{1}{2}$ to 1 minute until crisp and golden. Open basket; gently remove taco shell. Drain on paper towels. Repeat with remaining tortillas.

6. Layer beef, cheese, lettuce and tomato in each taco shell. Garnish, if desired.

Makes 6 servings

**Taco fryer baskets are available in large supermarkets and in housewares stores.

Step 1. Browning beef.

Step 3. Cooking beef until most of liquid has evaporated.

Step 5. Shaping tortilla into taco shell.

Pork Burritos

2 cups Refried Beans (page 152)
  or canned refried beans
1 boneless fresh pork butt roast
  (about 2½ pounds)
1 cup chopped white onion
1 carrot, sliced
1 clove garlic, minced
½ teaspoon salt
½ teaspoon ground cumin
½ teaspoon coriander seeds,
  lightly crushed
  Water
  Fresh Tomato Salsa (page 106)
12 flour tortillas (8-inch diameter)
2 medium, firm-ripe avocados,
  pared, pitted, diced
1 cup (4 ounces) shredded
  Monterey Jack cheese
  Carrot sticks, avocado slices
  and cilantro sprig for garnish

1. Prepare Refried Beans.

2. Place pork, white onion, sliced carrot, garlic, salt, cumin and coriander seeds in 5-quart Dutch oven. Add just enough water to cover pork. Bring to a boil over high heat. Reduce heat to low. Cover and simmer 2 to 2½ hours until pork is tender.

3. Prepare Fresh Tomato Salsa.

4. Preheat oven to 350°F. Remove pork from Dutch oven; set aside. Strain cooking liquid through cheesecloth-lined sieve; reserve ½ cup liquid.

5. Place pork on rack in roasting pan. Roast 40 to 45 minutes until well browned, turning once. Let stand until cool enough to handle.

6. Trim and discard outer fat from pork. Using 2 forks, pull pork into coarse shreds. Combine pork and reserved cooking liquid in medium skillet. Heat over medium heat 5 minutes or until meat is hot and moistly coated with liquid; stir often.

7. Soften and warm tortillas (technique on page 85). Reheat beans, if necessary.

8. Place about 2½ tablespoons beans on bottom half of 1 tortilla; spread out slightly. Layer with pork, salsa, diced avocado and cheese.

9. To form, fold right edge of tortilla up over filling; fold bottom edge over filling, then loosely roll up, leaving left end of burrito open. Garnish, if desired.

Makes 6 servings

Step 2. Adding enough water to cover pork.

Step 6. Pulling pork into coarse shreds.

Step 9. Forming burrito.

Spicy Grilled Chicken

1/3 cup Chili Butter (recipe follows)
6 boneless chicken breast halves
   (about 6 ounces each)
Jícama-Cucumber Salad
   (page 138) (optional)
Flour Tortillas (optional)

1. Prepare Chili Butter. Cut Chili Butter into 1/8-inch-thick slices. Loosen skin at one end of each chicken piece; insert 1 slice of Chili Butter under skin of each piece.

2. Preheat broiler. Place chicken, skin side down, on greased rack of broiler pan; dot with some of remaining butter. Broil chicken, 6 inches from heat, 10 minutes or until tops are browned. Turn chicken over; dot with more of the remaining butter. Broil 10 minutes or until browned and juices run clear.

3. To serve, top with Chili Butter, if desired. Serve with Jícama-Cucumber Salad and tortillas.   *Makes 6 servings*

Step 1. Placing Chili Butter under chicken skin.

Step 2. Dotting chicken with Chili Butter.

Chili Butter

1 small dried ancho chili, toasted, seeded,
   deveined, rinsed (page 85)
1 cup boiling water
1/2 cup butter, softened
1 clove garlic, minced
1/4 teaspoon dried oregano leaves, crushed

1. Place chili in small bowl; cover with boiling water. Let stand 1 hour.

2. Place chili and 1 1/2 tablespoons soaking water in blender; process until smooth. Cool completely. Discard remaining soaking water.

3. Beat butter in small bowl with electric mixer until fluffy. Beat in garlic and oregano. Gradually beat in chili mixture. Cover and refrigerate 30 minutes or until firm. Spoon butter in a strip onto plastic wrap; enclose in plastic wrap and roll back and forth to form smooth 1-inch-thick roll. Refrigerate until firm.   *Makes about 2/3 cup*

Chili Butter: Step 3. Rolling butter mixture into log.

Creamy Almond-Coated Chicken

1/2 cup blanched almonds
6 boneless skinless chicken breast halves (about 6 ounces each)
2 to 3 tablespoons vegetable oil, divided
1 tablespoon butter or margarine
1/4 cup finely chopped white onion
1 fresh Anaheim or poblano chili, roasted, peeled, seeded, deveined, finely chopped (pages 84–85)
1 small tomato, seeded, finely chopped (page 88)
1 clove garlic, minced
1/2 cup chicken broth
1/4 teaspoon salt
1/2 cup heavy cream
   Cilantro sprig for garnish
   Steamed sliced summer squash with chopped cilantro

1. Process almonds, about 1/4 at a time, with on/off pulses in electric spice grinder to fine powder. Place ground almonds on shallow plate.

2. Coat chicken with almonds; reserve remaining almonds.

3. Heat 1 tablespoon oil and butter in deep, large skillet over medium heat until foam subsides. Place breasts in single layer in skillet without crowding. Cook 6 minutes or until chicken is light brown, turning once. Reduce heat if almonds get too dark. Remove chicken to plate. Repeat with remaining chicken, adding 1 tablespoon of oil, if necessary.

4. Add remaining 1 tablespoon oil and onion to skillet. Cook and stir over medium heat 3 minutes or until onion is softened. Add chili, chopped tomato and garlic. Cook and stir 1 minute. Add broth, salt and reserved almonds. Bring to a boil over high heat.

5. Return chicken to skillet. Reduce heat to low. Cover and simmer 15 to 20 minutes until chicken is tender and juices run clear. Remove chicken to serving plate; cover and keep warm.

6. Add cream to broth mixture. Bring to a boil over medium-high heat. Cook and stir 3 to 5 minutes until sauce is slightly thickened. Pour over chicken. Garnish, if desired. Serve with summer squash. *Makes 6 servings*

Step 1. Placing ground almonds on plate.

Step 4. Cooking tomato mixture.

Step 5. Returning chicken to skillet.

Chicken Mole

3 small dried pasilla chilies, toasted, seeded, deveined, rinsed (page 85)
3 small dried mulato chilies, toasted, seeded, deveined, rinsed (page 85)
1½ cups boiling water
¼ cup sesame seeds
3 whole cloves
1 piece cinnamon stick (about 1 inch)
¼ teaspoon whole coriander seeds
⅛ teaspoon whole anise seeds
¼ cup vegetable oil
¼ cup whole unblanched almonds
¼ cup raisins
6 whole chicken legs, thighs attached (about 3 pounds)
¼ teaspoon salt
½ cup coarsely chopped white onion
2 cloves garlic
1 tablespoon tomato paste
1½ ounces Mexican chocolate
1 cup chicken broth
Tomato wedges and cilantro sprigs for garnish
Green Rice Pilaf (page 144) (optional)

1. Place pasilla and mulato chilies in medium bowl; cover with boiling water. Let stand 1 hour.

2. Toast sesame seeds in dry, heavy skillet over medium heat 2 minutes or until golden, stirring frequently. Remove from skillet.

3. Combine cloves, cinnamon stick, coriander seeds and anise seeds in same skillet; toast over medium heat 20 to 30 seconds until they start to change color and become fragrant, stirring frequently. Remove from skillet.

4. Heat oil in 12-inch skillet over medium heat until hot. Add almonds. Cook and stir 2 to 3 minutes until brown. Remove with slotted spoon; drain on paper towels.

5. Add raisins. Cook and stir 30 seconds or until puffed. Remove with slotted spoon.

6. Sprinkle chicken with salt. Cook in same skillet over medium heat 10 minutes or until browned, turning once. Remove to plate. Remove all but 2 tablespoons oil from skillet.

continued on page 120

Step 1. Covering chilies with boiling water.

Step 2. Toasting sesame seeds.

Step 4. Browning almonds.

Chicken Mole, continued

7. Place raisins in blender; process until finely ground. Coarsely chop almonds; add to blender. Process until finely ground. Add onion and garlic to blender; process until finely ground.

8. Process 2 tablespoons sesame seeds with on/off pulses in electric spice grinder to fine powder. Add to blender.

9. Process clove mixture in grinder to fine powder; add to blender.

10. Add chilies, ⅓ cup of the soaking water and the tomato paste to blender; process until smooth. If mixture is too thick, add just enough of the remaining soaking water, 1 teaspoon at a time, until blender blade can spin. Discard remaining soaking water.

11. Coarsely chop chocolate using a sharp knife.

12. Reheat oil in skillet over medium heat until hot. Reduce heat to medium-low. Add chili mixture. Cook and stir 5 minutes. Add chocolate; cook and stir 2 minutes or until melted. Gradually stir in broth. Cook and stir 5 minutes.

13. Return chicken to skillet. Reduce heat to low. Cover and simmer 45 minutes or until chicken is tender and juices run clear, turning chicken occasionally. Sprinkle remaining sesame seeds over chicken just before serving. Garnish, if desired. Serve with Green Rice Pilaf.   *Makes 6 servings*

Step 7. Adding onion to raisin mixture.

Step 10. Processed chili mixture.

Step 12. Cooking mole sauce.

Chilies Rellenos

Tomato Sauce (page 122)
8 fresh poblano or Anaheim
   chilies
  Picadillo Filling (page 122)
  Vegetable oil
$^1/_3$ cup all-purpose flour
 5 eggs, separated
$^1/_4$ teaspoon cream of tartar
$^1/_4$ teaspoon salt
  Pimiento-stuffed green olives
    for garnish

1. Prepare Tomato Sauce.

2. Roast, peel, seed and devein chilies leaving stems intact and taking care not to break chilies. (Technique on pages 84–85.)

3. Prepare Picadillo Filling.

4. Carefully spoon about $^1/_4$ cup Picadillo Filling into each chili; press chilies firmly between hands to ease out air and to close.

5. Preheat oven to 250°F. Heat 1 inch oil in deep, heavy skillet over medium-high heat to 375°F; adjust heat to maintain temperature. Line baking sheet with paper towels.

6. Roll each chili in flour to coat lightly; pat off excess. Reserve remaining flour, about $^1/_4$ cup.

7. Beat egg whites, cream of tartar and salt in large bowl with electric mixer at high speed until soft peaks form. Beat egg yolks in medium bowl with electric mixer at medium speed until thick and lemon colored. Gradually beat reserved flour into egg yolks until smooth. Fold $^1/_4$ of egg whites into yolk mixture; fold in remaining egg whites until blended.

8. To coat each chili with egg batter, grasp stems; support bottom of chili with fork. Dip into batter to coat; let excess drain off.

continued on page 122

Step 4. Spooning filling into chilies.

Step 6. Rolling chili in flour.

Step 8. Coating chili with egg batter.

Chilies Rellenos, continued

9. Immediately slip chili into oil. Fry 4 minutes or until deep gold, turning once. Remove with slotted spatula; drain on paper towels. Keep warm in oven.

10. Reheat Tomato Sauce over medium heat. Spoon sauce on plates; arrange chilies on plates. Garnish, if desired.
Makes 4 servings

Tomato Sauce

1½ pounds tomatoes, peeled, seeded (page 92)
  1 medium white onion, chopped
  1 clove garlic, chopped
  2 tablespoons vegetable oil
1½ cups chicken broth
  ½ teaspoon dried thyme leaves, crushed
  ¼ teaspoon salt

1. Place tomatoes, onion and garlic in blender; process until smooth.

2. Heat oil in deep, large skillet over medium heat until hot. Add tomato mixture; cook and stir 5 minutes.

3. Stir broth, thyme and salt into skillet. Bring to a boil over high heat. Reduce heat to medium-low. Cook and stir 10 to 15 minutes until sauce has thickened slightly. Remove from heat; set aside.
Makes about 2 cups

Picadillo Filling

  1 tablespoon vegetable oil
  ¼ cup slivered almonds
  ¾ pound ground beef
  ¼ cup finely chopped white onion
  1 large tomato, peeled, seeded, finely chopped (page 92)
  1 tablespoon tomato paste
  1 clove garlic, minced
  2 tablespoons raisins
  2 tablespoons thinly sliced pimiento-stuffed green olives
  1 tablespoon cider vinegar
  1 teaspoon dark brown sugar
  ¼ teaspoon salt
  ¼ teaspoon ground cinnamon
  ⅛ teaspoon ground cumin
  ⅛ teaspoon ground cloves

1. Heat oil in large skillet over medium heat. Add almonds; cook and stir 2 to 3 minutes until golden. Remove; drain on paper towels.

2. Crumble beef into skillet. Brown beef 5 minutes; stir often. Add onion; cook and stir 4 minutes or until softened. Add tomato, tomato paste and garlic. Cook and stir 2 minutes. Stir in remaining ingredients except almonds. Cover and simmer over low heat 15 minutes.

3. Uncover skillet; cook over medium-low 3 minutes until most of liquid has evaporated. Skim and discard fat. Stir in almonds. Let stand until cool enough to handle. *Makes about 2 cups*

Step 9. Frying chilies.

Picadillo Filling: Step 1. Toasting almonds.

Picadillo Filling: Step 2. Stirring spices into ground beef mixture.

Fajitas

2 beef skirt steaks (about 1 pound each)
2 cloves garlic, divided
3 tablespoons vegetable oil, divided
2 tablespoons *plus* 1 to 2 teaspoons fresh lime juice, divided
Dash ground black pepper
$\frac{1}{2}$ cup minced white onion
2 large tomatoes, seeded, finely chopped (page 88)
2 small green bell peppers, roasted, peeled, seeded, deveined, finely chopped (pages 84–85)
2 tablespoons minced cilantro
1 fresh serrano chili, minced
Refried Beans (page 152) (optional)
Flour Tortillas (8-inch diameter) (optional)

1. Place steaks between pieces of plastic wrap. Pound with flat side of meat mallet to $\frac{1}{4}$-inch thickness. Cut each steak crosswise into halves.

2. Pound 1 garlic clove with meat mallet to crush into coarse shreds. Combine with 2 tablespoons oil, 2 tablespoons lime juice and black pepper in large shallow glass baking dish. Add steaks, turning to coat with marinade. Marinate in refrigerator 30 minutes.

3. Mince remaining garlic clove. Cook and stir onion and garlic in remaining 1 tablespoon oil in medium skillet over medium heat 3 to 4 minutes until onion is softened. Remove from heat.

4. Stir in tomatoes, bell peppers, cilantro and chili. Season to taste with remaining lime juice. Let stand, covered, at room temperature.

5. Prepare coals for grill.* Remove steaks from marinade; pat dry with paper towels. Discard marinade. Grill 6 inches from heat 3 minutes for medium-rare or until desired doneness is reached, turning once.

6. Reheat beans, if necessary. If not freshly made, soften and warm tortillas (technique on page 85).

7. Serve steaks with tomato relish, Refried Beans and tortillas.   *Makes 4 servings*

*Steaks can be cooked on lightly oiled, well-seasoned heavy griddle or large skillet. Heat over medium heat until very hot. Cook steaks in single layer on griddle 3 minutes for medium-rare or until desired doneness is reached, turning once.

Step 1. Pounding meat to $\frac{1}{4}$-inch thickness.

Step 4. Stirring cilantro into tomato relish.

Chili

2 tablespoons vegetable oil
2 pounds ground chuck, coarse
    chili grind or regular grind
2 cups finely chopped white
    onions
1 or 2 dried de árbol chilies
2 cloves garlic, minced
1 teaspoon ground cumin
$^1\!/_2$ to 1 teaspoon salt
$^1\!/_4$ teaspoon ground cloves
1 can (28 ounces) whole peeled
    tomatoes, undrained, coarsely
    chopped
$^1\!/_2$ cup fresh orange juice
$^1\!/_2$ cup tequila or water
$^1\!/_4$ cup tomato paste
1 tablespoon grated orange peel
    Lime wedges and cilantro sprigs
    for garnish

1. Heat oil in deep, 12-inch skillet over medium-high heat until hot. Crumble beef into skillet. Brown beef 6 to 8 minutes, stirring to separate meat. Reduce heat to medium. Add onions. Cook and stir 5 minutes until onions are softened.

2. Crush chilies into fine flakes in mortar with pestle. Add chilies, garlic, cumin, salt and cloves to skillet. Cook and stir 30 seconds.

3. Stir in tomatoes, orange juice, tequila, tomato paste and orange peel. Bring to a boil over high heat. Reduce heat to low. Cover and simmer 1$^1\!/_2$ hours, stirring occasionally.

4. Uncover skillet. Cook chili over medium-low heat 10 to 15 minutes until thickened slightly, stirring frequently. Ladle into bowls. Garnish, if desired.   *Makes 6 to 8 servings*

Step 1. Browning ground beef.

Step 2. Crushing chilies in mortar with pestle.

Step 3. Stirring orange peel into tomato mixture.

Grilled Chili-Marinated Pork

3 tablespoons ground seeded dried pasilla chilies
1 teaspoon coarse or kosher salt
½ teaspoon ground cumin
2 tablespoons vegetable oil
1 tablespoon fresh lime juice
3 cloves garlic, minced
2 pounds pork tenderloin or thick boneless loin pork chops, trimmed of fat
Shredded romaine lettuce (optional)
Radishes for garnish

1. Mix chilies, salt and cumin in small bowl. Stir in oil and lime juice to make smooth paste. Stir in garlic.

2. Butterfly pork by cutting lengthwise about ⅔ of the way through, leaving meat in one piece; spread meat flat.

3. Cut tenderloin crosswise into 8 equal pieces. *Do not cut chops into pieces.*

4. Place pork between pieces of plastic wrap. Pound with flat side of meat mallet to ¼-inch thickness.

5. Spread chili paste on both sides of pork pieces to coat evenly. Place in shallow glass baking dish. Marinate, covered, in refrigerator 2 to 3 hours.

6. Prepare coals for grill or preheat broiler. Grill or broil pork 6 inches from heat 8 to 10 minutes for grilling or 6 to 7 minutes for broiling, turning once. Serve on lettuce-lined plate. Garnish, if desired.

Makes 6 to 8 servings

Step 2. Butterflying pork roast.

Step 3. Cutting pork roast into 8 equal pieces.

Step 4. Pounding meat to ¼-inch thickness.

Pork Stew

2 tablespoons vegetable oil
3 pounds lean, fresh boneless
  pork butt, cut into 1¹/₂-inch
  cubes
2 medium white onions, cut
  lengthwise into thin slices
3 cloves garlic, minced
1 teaspoon salt
1 teaspoon ground cumin
³/₄ teaspoon dried oregano leaves,
  crushed
1 cup fresh tomatillos, husked, *or*
  1 can (8 ounces) tomatillos,
  drained and chopped
3 or 4 fresh Anaheim chilies *or*
  1 can (4 ounces) green chilies,
  seeded, deveined, finely
  chopped
1 large tomato, peeled, coarsely
  chopped (page 92)
¹/₄ cup cilantro
³/₄ cup chicken broth
 2 teaspoons fresh lime juice
 4 cups hot cooked white rice
¹/₂ cup toasted slivered almonds
  (page 122)
  Cilantro sprigs and radish slices
  for garnish

1. Heat oil in 5-quart Dutch oven over medium heat until hot. Brown pork, about ¹/₃ at a time, in single layer in hot oil 10 minutes, turning occasionally. Remove to plate. Repeat with remaining pork.

2. Remove and discard all but 2 tablespoons drippings from pan. Add onions and garlic. Cook and stir 4 minutes or until onions are soft. Stir in salt, cumin and oregano.

3. Add tomatillos, chilies, tomato and cilantro. Stir in broth. Bring to a boil over high heat.

4. Return pork to pan. Reduce heat to low. Cover and simmer 1¹/₂ to 2 hours until pork is tender.

5. Uncover pan. Increase heat to medium. Cook at a low boil 20 to 30 minutes until sauce is thickened, stirring occasionally. Stir in lime juice.

6. Serve pork stew over rice; sprinkle with almonds. Garnish, if desired.

Makes 10 to 12 servings

Step 1. Browning pork.

Step 2. Cooking onions.

Step 3. Stirring broth into vegetable mixture.

Red Snapper in Chili-Tomato Sauce

6 red snapper fillets (8 to
    10 ounces each)
¼ teaspoon salt
⅛ teaspoon pepper
⅓ cup all-purpose flour
¼ cup olive oil
 3 cloves garlic, sliced
 2 medium white onions, cut
    lengthwise into thin slivers
1½ pounds fresh plum tomatoes,
    peeled, seeded, finely chopped
    (page 92)
½ cup tomato juice
¼ cup fresh lime juice
¼ cup sliced pimiento-stuffed
    green olives
 1 or 2 pickled jalapeño chilies,
    seeded, finely chopped
 1 tablespoon drained capers
 1 bay leaf
    Fresh bay leaves and lime slices
    for garnish
    Boiled, quartered new potatoes
    with fresh dill (optional)

1. Sprinkle fish with salt and pepper. Coat both sides of fish with flour; shake off excess.

2. Heat oil in 12-inch skillet over medium heat. Add garlic; cook and stir 2 to 3 minutes until golden. Remove garlic with slotted spoon; discard.

3. Place fillets in single layer in skillet without crowding. Cook over medium heat 4 minutes or until fillets are light brown, turning once. Remove to plate. Repeat with remaining fillets.

4. Add onions. Cook and stir 4 minutes or until onions are softened. Stir in tomatoes, tomato juice, lime juice, olives, chilies, capers and bay leaf. Bring to a boil over high heat. Reduce heat to low. Cover and simmer 15 minutes.

5. Add any accumulated juices from fillets on plate to skillet. Increase heat to medium-high. Cook, uncovered, 2 to 3 minutes until thickened, stirring frequently. Remove and discard bay leaf.

6. Return fillets to skillet. Spoon sauce over fillets. Reduce heat to low. Cover; simmer 3 to 5 minutes until fillets flake easily when tested with a fork. Garnish, if desired. Serve with potatoes. *Makes 6 servings*

Step 1. Coating fish with flour.

Step 2. Removing garlic from skillet.

Step 4. Stirring in remaining sauce ingredients.

Baked Fish Steaks

1 tablespoon annatto seeds
1 cup boiling water
1½ tablespoons orange juice
1½ tablespoons cider vinegar
2 cloves garlic, chopped
1 small dried de árbol chili,
coarsely crumbled
¾ teaspoon ground cumin
½ teaspoon ground allspice
¼ teaspoon salt
⅛ teaspoon pepper
4 pieces fresh halibut steaks or
mackerel or sea bass fillets
(about 8 ounces each)
Vegetable oil
Sliced green onions
Orange peel for garnish

1. Place annatto seeds in small bowl; cover with boiling water. Let stand, covered, at room temperature at least 8 hours or overnight.

2. Drain annatto seeds; discard liquid. Place annatto seeds, orange juice, vinegar, garlic, chili, cumin, allspice, salt and pepper in blender; process until smooth.

3. Spread annatto paste over both sides of fish to coat. Arrange fish in single layer in well-oiled baking dish. Cover and refrigerate 1 to 2 hours to blend flavors.

4. Preheat oven to 350°F. Bake fish, uncovered, 20 to 25 minutes until fish flakes easily when tested with fork. Sprinkle green onions over tops before serving. Garnish, if desired. *Makes 4 servings*

Step 1. Covering annatto seeds with boiling water.

Step 2. Adding annatto paste ingredients to blender.

Step 3. Arranging fish in baking dish.

Baked Shrimp with Chili-Garlic Butter

1½ pounds medium raw shrimp in
    shells
½ cup butter
¼ cup vegetable oil
8 cloves garlic, finely chopped
1 to 3 dried de árbol chilies,
    coarsely crumbled*
1 tablespoon fresh lime juice
¼ teaspoon salt
    Green onion tops, slivered, for
    garnish

*For milder flavor, seed some or all of the
chilies.

1. Preheat oven to 400°F. Shell and devein shrimp, leaving tails attached; rinse and drain well.

2. Heat butter and oil in small skillet over medium heat until butter is melted and foamy. Add garlic, chilies, lime juice and salt. Cook and stir 1 minute. Remove from heat.

3. Arrange shrimp in even layer in shallow 2-quart gratin pan or baking dish. Pour hot butter mixture over shrimp.

4. Bake shrimp 10 to 12 minutes until shrimp turn pink and opaque, stirring once. Do not overcook or shrimp will be dry and tough. Garnish, if desired.   *Makes 4 servings*

Step 1. Removing shells from shrimp.

Step 2. Adding seasonings to melted butter.

Step 3. Pouring butter mixture over shrimp.

Jícama-Cucumber Salad

1 jícama (1¼ to 1½ pounds)*
1 small cucumber, unpared
½ cup very thinly slivered mild red onion
2 tablespoons fresh lime juice
½ teaspoon grated lime peel
1 clove garlic, minced
¼ teaspoon salt
⅛ teaspoon crumbled dried de árbol chili
3 tablespoons vegetable oil
Leaf lettuce
Red onion slivers and lime wedges for garnish

*Or, substitute Jerusalem artichokes. Cut pared artichokes lengthwise into halves; cut halves crosswise into thin slices.

1. Pare jícama. Cut lengthwise into 8 wedges; cut wedges crosswise into ⅛-inch-thick slices.

2. Cut cucumber lengthwise in half; scoop out and discard seeds. Cut halves crosswise into ⅛-inch-thick slices.

3. Combine jícama, cucumber and onion in large bowl; toss lightly to mix.

4. Combine lime juice, lime peel, garlic, salt and chili in small bowl. Gradually add oil, whisking continuously, until dressing is thoroughly blended.

5. Pour dressing over salad; toss lightly to coat. Cover and refrigerate 1 to 2 hours to blend flavors.

6. Serve salad in lettuce-lined salad bowl. Garnish, if desired.   *Makes 6 servings*

Step 1. Cutting jícama crosswise into ⅛-inch-thick slices.

Step 2. Removing seeds from cucumber half.

Step 5. Pouring dressing over salad.

Zesty Zucchini-Chick Pea Salad

3 medium zucchini (about
  6 ounces each)
$\frac{1}{2}$ teaspoon salt
5 tablespoons white vinegar
1 clove garlic, minced
$\frac{1}{4}$ teaspoon dried thyme leaves,
  crushed
$\frac{1}{2}$ cup olive oil
1 cup drained canned chick peas
$\frac{1}{2}$ cup sliced pitted ripe olives
3 green onions, minced
1 canned chipotle chili in adobo
  sauce, drained, seeded, minced
1 ripe avocado, pitted, pared, cut
  into $\frac{1}{2}$-inch cubes
$\frac{1}{3}$ cup crumbled feta *or* 3
  tablespoons grated Romano
  cheese
1 head Boston lettuce, cored,
  separated into leaves
  Sliced tomatoes and cilantro
  sprigs for garnish

1. Cut zucchini lengthwise into halves; cut halves crosswise into $\frac{1}{4}$-inch-thick slices. Place slices in medium bowl; sprinkle with salt. Toss to mix. Spread zucchini on several layers of paper towels. Let stand at room temperature 30 minutes to drain.

2. Combine vinegar, garlic and thyme in large bowl. Gradually add oil, whisking continuously until dressing is thoroughly blended.

3. Pat zucchini dry; add to dressing. Add chick peas, olives and onions; toss lightly to coat. Cover and refrigerate at least 30 minutes or up to 4 hours, stirring occasionally.

4. Add chili to salad just before serving. Stir gently to mix. Add avocado and cheese; toss lightly to mix.

5. Serve salad in lettuce-lined shallow bowl or plate. Garnish, if desired.

Makes 4 to 6 servings

Step 1. Draining zucchini on paper towels.

Step 2. Whisking oil into vinegar mixture.

Step 4. Adding avocado and cheese to salad.

Arroz Rojos

2 tablespoons vegetable oil
1 cup raw long-grain white rice
   (not converted)
½ cup finely chopped white onion
1 clove garlic, minced
½ teaspoon salt
½ teaspoon ground cumin
   Dash chili powder
2 large tomatoes, peeled, seeded,
   chopped (page 92)
1½ cups chicken broth
  ⅓ cup shelled fresh or thawed
    frozen peas
2 tablespoons chopped pimiento
   Red pepper arrows for garnish*

*To make red pepper arrows, cut a
½-inch-wide strip from a red pepper.
Make a V-shaped cut in strip at 1-inch
intervals.

1. Heat oil in medium skillet over medium heat until hot. Add rice. Cook and stir 2 minutes or until rice turns opaque.

2. Add onion; cook and stir 1 minute. Stir in garlic, salt, cumin and chili powder. Add tomatoes; cook and stir 2 minutes.

3. Stir in broth. Bring to a boil over high heat. Reduce heat to low. Cover and simmer 15 minutes or until rice is almost tender.

4. Stir in peas and chopped pimiento. Cover and cook 2 to 4 minutes until rice is tender and all liquid has been absorbed. Rice grains will be slightly firm and separate, rather than soft and sticky. Garnish, if desired.

Makes 4 to 6 servings

Step 1. Cooking rice until it turns opaque.

Step 2. Cooking tomatoes in rice mixture.

Step 4. Adding remaining ingredients to rice mixture.

Green Rice Pilaf

2 tablespoons vegetable oil
1 cup raw long-grain white rice
    (not converted)
¼ cup finely chopped white onion
2 fresh poblano or Anaheim
    chilies, roasted, peeled,
    seeded, deveined, chopped
    (pages 84–85)
6 thin green onions, thinly sliced
1 clove garlic, minced
¼ teaspoon salt
¼ teaspoon ground cumin
1¾ cups chicken broth
1½ cups shredded queso Chihuahua
    or Monterey Jack cheese
⅓ cup coarsely chopped cilantro
    Cilantro sprig for garnish

1. Preheat oven to 375°F. Heat oil in large skillet over medium heat until hot. Add rice. Cook and stir 2 minutes or until rice turns opaque.

2. Add white onion; cook and stir 1 minute. Stir in chilies, green onions, garlic, salt and cumin; cook and stir 20 seconds.

3. Stir in broth. Bring to a boil over high heat. Reduce heat to low. Cover and simmer 15 minutes or until rice is almost tender.*

4. Remove skillet from heat. Add 1 cup cheese and chopped cilantro; toss lightly to mix. Transfer to greased 1½-quart baking dish; top with remaining ½ cup cheese.

5. Bake, uncovered, 15 minutes or until rice is tender and cheese topping is melted. Garnish, if desired.   *Makes 4 to 6 servings*

*For plain green rice, complete recipe from this point as follows: Cook rice in skillet 2 to 4 minutes more until tender. Stir in chopped cilantro just before serving; omit cheese.

Step 2. Stirring chilies, onions and seasonings into rice mixture.

Step 3. Mixing broth into rice mixture.

Step 4. Tossing cheese with rice mixture.

Caramel Flan

1 cup sugar, divided
2 cups half-and-half
1 cup milk
1½ teaspoons vanilla extract
6 eggs
2 egg yolks
Hot water
Fresh strawberries for garnish

1. Preheat oven to 325°F. Heat 5½- to 6-cup ring mold in oven 10 minutes or until hot.

2. Heat ½ cup sugar in heavy, medium skillet over medium-high heat 5 to 8 minutes or until sugar is completely melted and deep amber color, stirring frequently. *Do not allow sugar to burn.*

3. Immediately pour caramelized sugar into ring mold. Holding mold with potholder, quickly rotate to coat bottom and sides evenly with sugar. Place mold on wire rack. (**Caution:** Caramelized sugar is very hot; do not touch it.)

4. Combine half-and-half and milk in heavy 2-quart saucepan. Heat over medium heat until almost simmering; remove from heat. Add remaining ½ cup sugar and vanilla, stirring until sugar is dissolved.

5. Lightly beat eggs and egg yolks in large bowl until blended but not foamy; gradually stir in milk mixture. Pour custard into ring mold.

6. Place mold in large baking pan; pour hot water into baking pan to depth of ½ inch. Bake 35 to 40 minutes until knife inserted into center of custard comes out clean.

7. Remove mold from water bath; place on wire rack. Let stand 30 minutes. Cover and refrigerate 1½ to 2 hours until thoroughly chilled.

8. To serve, loosen inner and outer edges of flan with tip of small knife. Cover mold with rimmed serving plate; invert and lift off mold. Garnish, if desired. Spoon some of the melted caramel over each serving.

Makes 6 to 8 servings

Step 2. Melting sugar in skillet.

Step 3. Coating mold with hot caramelized sugar.

Step 6. Inserting knife to test for doneness.

Mexican Fritters

1 cup water
½ cup butter or margarine
⅓ cup *plus* 1 teaspoon sugar,
  divided
¼ teaspoon salt
¼ teaspoon ground nutmeg
1 cup all-purpose flour
4 eggs
½ teaspoon vanilla extract
  Vegetable oil

1. Combine water, butter, 1 teaspoon sugar, salt and nutmeg in 2-quart saucepan. Heat over medium-high heat until butter is melted, stirring occasionally. Increase heat to high. Bring to a full rolling boil.

2. Add flour all at once to saucepan; remove from heat. Beat with wooden spoon until mixture forms smooth, thick paste. Cook and stir over medium-high heat 1 to 2 minutes until mixture pulls away from side of pan and forms a ball and a film forms on bottom of pan.

3. Add eggs, 1 at a time, beating vigorously after each addition until dough is smooth and shiny. Stir in vanilla. Let dough stand at room temperature 15 minutes.

4. Heat 1 inch oil in deep, heavy, large skillet over medium-high heat to 375°F; adjust heat to maintain temperature. Line baking sheet with paper towels.

5. Spoon dough into pastry bag or cookie press fitted with large star tip (about ½ inch).

6. Carefully press dough directly into hot oil in 6-inch-long strips, cutting strips with scissors to detach. Fry strips, 3 or 4 at a time, 5 to 7 minutes until brown, turning once. Gently remove with tongs or slotted spoon; drain well on paper towels. Repeat until all dough has been fried.

7. Roll warm strips in remaining ⅓ cup sugar to coat lightly.   *Makes about 18 strips*

Step 2. Beating flour into butter mixture until it forms a thick paste.

Step 3. Beating in eggs until dough is smooth and shiny.

Step 6. Cutting dough strips with scissors.

Chocolate-Rum Parfaits

6 to 6 ¹/₂ ounces Mexican
   chocolate
1 ¹/₂ cups heavy cream, divided
3 tablespoons golden rum
   (optional)
³/₄ teaspoon vanilla
   Sliced almonds for garnish
   Cookies (optional)

1. Coarsely chop chocolate using a sharp knife.

2. Combine chocolate and 3 tablespoons heavy cream in top of double boiler. Heat over simmering water until smooth, stirring occasionally. Gradually stir in rum; remove from water. Let stand at room temperature 15 minutes to cool slightly.

3. Combine remaining cream and vanilla in chilled small bowl. Beat with electric mixer at low speed, then gradually increase speed until cream is stiff, but not chunky.

4. Gently fold whipped cream into cooled chocolate mixture until uniform in color. Spoon mousse into 4 individual dessert dishes. Refrigerate 2 to 3 hours until firm. Garnish, if desired. Serve with cookies.

Makes 4 servings

Step 1. Coarsely chopping chocolate.

Step 3. Beating cream and vanilla.

Step 4. Folding whipped cream into cooled chocolate.

Refried Beans

8 ounces dried red, pink or pinto beans (1⅓ cups)
4½ cups cold water
⅓ cup *plus* 1 tablespoon vegetable shortening or vegetable oil, divided
1 small white onion, sliced
1½ teaspoons salt
1 small white onion, finely chopped
1 small clove garlic, minced

1. Rinse beans thoroughly in sieve under cold running water, picking out any debris or blemished beans.

2. Place beans, water, 1 tablespoon shortening and sliced onion in 3-quart saucepan. Bring to a boil over high heat. Reduce heat to low. Cover and simmer 1½ hours or just until beans are tender, not soft.

3. Stir in salt. Cover and simmer over very low heat 30 to 45 minutes until beans are very soft. Do not drain.*

4. Heat remaining ⅓ cup shortening in heavy, large skillet over high heat until very hot. Add chopped onion and garlic. Reduce heat to medium. Cook and stir 4 minutes or until onion is softened.

5. Increase heat to high. Add 1 cup undrained beans. Cook and stir, mashing beans with bean or potato masher.

6. As beans begin to dry, add another 1 cup undrained beans. Cook and stir, mashing beans with bean or potato masher. Repeat until all beans and cooking liquid have been added and mixture is a coarse purée. Adjust heat as needed to prevent beans from sticking and burning. Total cooking time will be around 20 minutes.

7. Beans may be served as a side dish or used as an ingredient for another recipe.

Makes about 2 cups

*Flavor is improved if beans are prepared to this point, then refrigerated, covered, overnight before completing recipe.

Step 1. Rinsing beans.

Step 5. Mashing beans.

Step 6. Adding cooking liquid to mashed beans.

Flour Tortillas

2 cups all-purpose flour
$\frac{1}{2}$ teaspoon salt
$\frac{1}{4}$ cup vegetable shortening
$\frac{1}{2}$ cup warm water

1. Combine flour and salt in medium bowl. Rub shortening into flour with fingertips until mixture has fine, even texture. Stir in water until dough forms.

2. Knead dough on floured surface 2 to 3 minutes until smooth and elastic. Wrap in plastic wrap. Let stand 30 minutes at room temperature.

3. Knead dough a few times. Divide evenly into 8 pieces for 10-inch tortillas or 12 pieces for 8-inch tortillas. Shape pieces into balls; cover with plastic wrap to prevent them from drying out.

4. Using rolling pin, roll out each dough ball on floured surface, turning over frequently, into 8- or 10-inch circle. Stack each tortilla between sheets of waxed paper.

5. Heat ungreased heavy griddle or skillet over medium-high heat until a little water sprinkled on surface dances. Carefully lay 1 tortilla on griddle; cook 20 to 30 seconds until top is bubbly and bottom is flecked with brown spots. Turn tortilla over; cook 15 to 20 seconds until flecked with brown spots. If tortilla puffs up while second side is cooking, press it down gently with spatula. Remove tortilla to foil.

6. Cook remaining tortillas as directed in step 5. If griddle becomes too hot, reduce heat to prevent burning. Stack cooked tortillas and cover with foil until all are cooked. Use immediately or wrap in foil and keep warm in 250°F oven up to 30 minutes. Tortillas are best when fresh, but can be wrapped in foil and refrigerated up to 3 days or frozen up to 2 weeks. Reheat in 350°F oven 10 minutes before using.

Makes 8 (10-inch) or 12 (8-inch) tortillas

Step 2. Kneading dough.

Step 4. Rolling dough into circle.

Step 5. Pressing tortilla down to flatten puffed area.

Corn Tortillas

2 cups masa harina
1 to 1¼ cups warm water
  Corn Tortilla Chips (page 155)

1. Cut 2 (7-inch) squares from heavy-duty plastic bag. Combine masa harina and 1 cup water in medium bowl. Add remaining water, 1 tablespoon at a time, until a smooth stiff dough is formed.

2. Test consistency of dough by rolling 1 piece dough into 1¾-inch ball; flatten slightly. Place ball on piece of plastic on lower plate of tortilla press, slightly off-center away from handle.* Cover with second piece of plastic; press down firmly with top of press to make 6-inch tortilla. Peel off top piece of plastic; invert tortilla onto hand and peel off second piece of plastic. If edges are cracked or ragged, dough is too dry; mix in water, 1 to 2 teaspoons at a time, until dough presses out with smooth edges. If tortilla sticks to plastic, dough is too wet; mix in masa harina, 1 tablespoon at a time, until dough no longer sticks when pressed.

3. When dough has correct consistency, divide evenly into 12 pieces for 6-inch tortillas or 24 pieces for 4-inch tortillas. Shape pieces into balls; cover with plastic wrap to prevent them from drying out.

4. Press out tortillas as directed in step 2, stacking between sheets of plastic wrap or waxed paper.

Step 1. Adding water, 1 tablespoon at a time, to dough.

Step 2. Flattening dough in tortilla press.

Step 2. Testing texture of flattened dough.

5. Heat ungreased heavy griddle or skillet over medium-high heat until a little water sprinkled on surface dances. Carefully lay 1 tortilla on griddle; cook 30 seconds or until edges begin to dry out. Turn tortilla over; cook 45 seconds to 1 minute until dry and lightly flecked with brown spots. Turn tortilla over again; cook first side 15 to 20 seconds more until dry and light brown. During last stage of cooking, tortilla may puff up; do not press down. Remove tortilla to kitchen towel; it will be slightly stiff, but will soften as it stands.

6. Cook remaining tortillas as directed in step 5. If griddle becomes too hot, reduce heat to prevent burning. Stack cooked tortillas and keep wrapped in towel until all are cooked. Use immediately or wrap in foil and keep warm in 250°F oven up to 30 minutes. Tortillas are best when fresh, but can be wrapped in foil and refrigerated up to 3 days or frozen up to 2 weeks. Reheat in 350°F oven 10 minutes before using.

*Makes 12 (6-inch) or
24 (4-inch) tortillas*

*A tortilla press works best, but if necessary, you can press with bottom of pie plate or heavy skillet.

Corn Tortilla Chips

**12 corn tortillas (6-inch diameter),
preferably day-old
Vegetable oil
$^1/_2$ to 1 teaspoon salt**

1. If tortillas are fresh, let stand, uncovered, in single layer on wire rack 1 to 2 hours to dry slightly.

2. Stack 6 tortillas; cutting through stack, cut tortillas into 6 or 8 equal wedges. Repeat with remaining tortillas.

3. Heat $^1/_2$ inch oil in deep, heavy, large skillet over medium-high heat to 375°F; adjust heat to maintain temperature.

4. Fry tortilla wedges in a single layer 1 minute or until crisp, turning occasionally. Remove with slotted spoon; drain on paper towels. Repeat until all chips have been fried. Sprinkle chips with salt.

Makes 6 to 8 dozen chips

Note: Tortilla chips are served with salsa as a snack, used as the base for nachos and used as scoops for guacamole, other dips or refried beans. They are best eaten fresh, but can be stored, tightly covered, in cool place 2 or 3 days. Reheat in 350°F oven a few minutes before serving.

Step 5. Cooking tortilla.

Corn Tortilla Chips: Step 2. Cutting tortillas into chips.

Corn Tortilla Chips: Step 4. Frying chips.

STEP-BY-STEP COOKING

CHINESE

Honey-Glazed Spareribs *(page 186)*

CLASS NOTES

TECHNIQUES FOR CHINESE COOKING

Preparing tasty and attractive Chinese dishes can be a rewarding experience that is easy to accomplish. There are just a few rules to keep in mind for successfully cooking most recipes: 1) Preparation and cooking are two separate procedures. 2) All ingredients should be prepared *before* any cooking is begun. 3) Paying attention to the cooking process is crucial because many of the foods are cooked over intense heat in a matter of minutes.

The Chinese have perfected a variety of cooking techniques, including stir-frying, deep-frying, braising, stewing, steaming, roasting, barbecuing and preserving. All of these techniques are probably familiar to you. But in order to stir-fry correctly, an understanding of its basic principles is necessary.

Stir-frying—a rapid-cooking method invented by the Chinese—is the brisk cooking of small pieces of ingredients in hot oil over intense heat for a short time, usually just for a few minutes. During cooking, the ingredients must be kept in constant motion by stirring or tossing vigorously. Once cooking is completed, the food should be removed immediately from heat.

When stir-frying, all of the ingredients must be well organized and prepared *before the cooking is started*. They should be measured or weighed, cleaned, chopped, sliced, combined or the like. Meat, poultry, fish and vegetables should be cut into pieces of approximately the same size for even cooking. Otherwise, one ingredient may be overcooked while others remain undercooked. The stir-frying is accomplished so quickly that there is usually not time to complete any preparation steps once cooking is begun.

The intensity of the heat used for stir-frying is important. In most cases, easily controlled high heat is needed. For this reason, a gas range with its ability for instant heat control is generally more efficient for stir-frying than is an electric range.

The kind of oil used is also crucial. A vegetable oil that can be heated to a high temperature without smoking is essential. Peanut oil, corn oil, cottonseed oil and soybean oil all work well. Other kinds of fats, such as olive oil, sesame oil, butter or lard cannot be used because they have low burning points.

Due to the variables involved in stir-frying, such as kinds of foods, type of heat and the kind of

cooking equipment used, cooking times given in this publication should be used as guidelines—not as absolutes. Most of the recipes, for example, were tested on a gas range. Cooking times needed when using a wok on an electric range, or when using an electric wok, may vary somewhat.

UTENSILS FOR CHINESE COOKING

A reasonably equipped kitchen usually contains more than enough utensils to adequately handle Chinese cooking. However, one item you may not have, but may wish to consider purchasing, is a wok, especially if you plan to make stir-fried dishes often. Invented many centuries ago, the wok is an all-purpose cooking pan used in virtually every Chinese household for almost every kind of cooking.

Traditionally, a wok was made from thin, tempered iron, and had a rounded bottom for fast, even conduction of heat. However, modern technology has brought some changes to the wok. In addition to iron, woks are now manufactured in aluminum, stainless steel and carbon steel. Woks with flat bottoms are made for use on electric ranges and on smooth-top cooking surfaces. There are electric woks with nonstick finishes and automatic thermostatic controls. On some woks, the customary thin metal handles positioned on two sides have been replaced with a single long wooden handle. This version eliminates the necessity of keeping pot holders handy at all times to pick up or steady the wok.

Woks range in size from 12 to 24 inches in diameter. The 14-inch size is a good choice because it can handle most stir-frying and other cooking chores without interfering with the use of other burners on the range top.

Before a new iron or carbon steel wok is used, it should be washed and seasoned. Wash it thoroughly in hot, soapy water (the first time only) and use a scouring pad, if necessary, to remove any protective coating. Rinse the wok with water and dry it completely. Rub 1 tablespoon of vegetable oil completely over the interior of the wok. Place it over low heat until hot throughout, 3 to 5 minutes; remove wok from heat and let cool.

After each use, the wok should be soaked in hot water and cleaned with a bamboo brush or a sponge. Do not clean the wok with soap or soap-treated scouring pads. Rinse the wok with water, dry it and place over low heat until all water evaporates. Then rub 1 teaspoon of vegetable oil over the inside of the wok to prevent it from rusting.

Another very useful utensil for Chinese cooking is a cleaver. While not essential, it is handy for slicing, chopping and mincing ingredients, and is especially helpful for chopping whole chickens into Chinese-style serving pieces (see page 195).

INGREDIENTS IN CHINESE CUISINE

When preparing Chinese foods, you will come across many ingredients that are familiar. You will also encounter some that may be unfamiliar such as wood ears, oyster sauce or Chinese five-spice powder. Some of the items—seasonings in particular—may be available only in Chinese food markets. Before you search for an out-of-the-way specialty store, however, check your local supermarket. Many supermarkets now stock good inventories of Chinese ingredients. In addition to canned, bottled or packaged goods, many carry fresh items such as Chinese cabbage (napa or bok choy), bean sprouts, wonton and egg-roll wrappers, bean curd and Chinese-style thin egg noodles. A check of the frozen-food cases will yield additional Chinese items.

As with any other kind of cooking, choose the freshest ingredients you can find, especially when purchasing vegetables, meat, poultry or fish. The Chinese are so conscientious about cooking with the freshest possible foods that they plan their menus around the foods they find in the market—rather than planning the marketing around the menu.

The glossary that follows describes many of the Chinese foods used in the recipes in this publication.

GLOSSARY OF CHINESE INGREDIENTS

Bamboo shoots: tender, ivory-colored shoots of tropical bamboo plants, used separately as a vegetable and to add crispness and a slight sweetness to dishes. They are available in cans—whole or sliced—and should be rinsed with water before using.

Bean curd (also called tofu): puréed soybeans pressed to form a white custardlike cake, used as a vegetable and as an excellent source of protein. Bean curd can be used in all kinds of recipes because it readily absorbs the flavor of other foods. Bean curd is available fresh or in cans. If fresh, it should be covered with water and stored in the refrigerator.

Bean sauce (also called yellow bean sauce or brown bean sauce): a Chinese seasoning made from soybeans, flour, vinegar, salt and spices such as hot chilies.

Bean sprouts: small white shoots of the pea-like mung bean plant, used separately as a vegetable and included in a wide variety of dishes. They are available fresh or in cans. Canned sprouts should be rinsed before use to eliminate any metallic taste. Fresh or opened, unused canned sprouts should be covered with water and stored in the refrigerator.

Bean threads (also called Chinese rice vermicelli, transparent or cellophane noodles): dry, hard, white, fine noodles made from powdered mung beans. They have little flavor of their own, but readily absorb the flavors of other foods. Bean threads can be used in numerous steamed, simmered, deep-fried or stir-fried dishes. They are available in packets or small bundles.

Cabbage, Chinese: there are two types of Chinese cabbages generally available in American markets. One is bok choy, which has white stalks and green, crinkled leaves. The other is napa cabbage, which has elongated tightly furled leaves with wide white ribs and soft pale green tips. Both varieties need very little cooking and are often included in soups and stir-fried dishes.

Chili oil (also called chili pepper oil or hot pepper oil): reddish colored, fiery hot oil made from peanut oil infused with dried red chili peppers. Use sparingly for flavoring. Store in cool, dark place.

Chili peppers: smooth-skinned, pungent pods that play an important role in the cuisines of many countries, including China. There are more than 200 varieties, which vary from mildly warm to blistering hot.

Chili sauce, Chinese: a bright red, extremely spicy sauce made from crushed fresh chili peppers and salt. It is available in cans or bottles and should be used sparingly.

Chives, Chinese (also called garlic chives): thin, slender, flat green leaves give a distinctive garlic flavor to many Chinese dishes.

Corn, baby: 2- to 3-inch-long yellow ears of corn with tiny kernels. The edible cobs are slightly sweet tasting and crunchy. Available in cans or jars packed in salted water, drain or rinse with cold water to remove brine before using. Store, covered with water in jar, in refrigerator up to 1½ weeks; change water every 2 days.

Egg noodles, Chinese-style: thin pasta usually made of flour, egg, water and salt. The noodles can be purchased fresh, frozen or dehydrated. They can be boiled, braised, stir-fried or deep-fried; the time and method of cooking vary with the type of noodle. Check the package for specific instructions.

Five-spice powder, Chinese: cocoa-colored, ready-mixed blend of five ground spices, usually anise seed, fennel, clove, cinnamon and ginger or pepper. It has a slightly sweet, pungent flavor and should be used sparingly.

Ginger (also called gingerroot): a knobby, gnarled root, having a brown skin and whitish or light green interior. It has a fresh, pungent flavor and is used as a basic seasoning in many Chinese recipes. Ginger is available fresh or in cans. It will keep for weeks in the refrigerator wrapped in plastic, or for months if kept in salted water or dry sherry. Always remove the outer brown skin from fresh ginger before using in any recipe.

Hoisin sauce: a thick, dark brown sauce made of soybeans, flour, sugar, spices, garlic, chili and salt. It has a sweet, spicy flavor and is called for in numerous Chinese recipes.

Lychee (also called lichee or litchi): a small, juicy, oval-shaped fruit with a brownish or bright red skin, white pulp and large pit. It is used in main dishes in combination with other foods or served separately as a dessert or snack. Lychees are available in cans whole, pitted and packed in syrup.

Mushrooms, dried: dehydrated black or brown mushrooms from the Orient, having caps from 1 to 3 inches in diameter. They have a strong, distinctive flavor and are included in many different kinds of recipes. Chinese dried mushrooms must be soaked in hot water before using; they are usually thinly sliced prior to combining them with other foods. Dried mushrooms are available in cellophane packages.

Mushrooms, Fresh Shiitake: large, dark brown mushrooms with meaty caps that have a rich flavor. The average size is about 3 inches in diameter; however, some are as large as 10 inches across. Refrigerate, unwashed, in a ventilated package or a plastic bag punched with holes up to five days. Use as soon as possible for best flavor.

Mushrooms, Straw: dark brown, pointed cap mushrooms with squat yellowish-tan stems. They are about 1 inch in diameter and have a mild delicate flavor and silky texture. They are available canned; drain and rinse before using.

Oyster sauce: a thick, brown, concentrated sauce made of ground oysters, soy sauce and brine. It imparts very little fish flavor and is used as a seasoning to intensify other flavors. Oyster sauce is included in a variety of recipes, especially in stir-fried Cantonese dishes.

Parsley, Chinese (also called cilantro or fresh coriander): a strongly flavored green herb with flat broad leaves similar in appearance to Italian or flat-leaf parsley. Commonly used fresh as a seasoning or garnish.

Plum sauce: a thick, piquant chutney-like sauce frequently served with duck or pork dishes. It is available in cans or bottles.

Rice sticks (also called rice noodles): *flat* noodles made from rice flour and available in thin, medium and wide widths. They are off-white in color, opaque and brittle. Soften the noodles in warm water before using, unless frying them in oil. They keep indefinitely in a tightly covered container in a cool, dry place. Rice vermicelli, available in several widths in packets or small bundles, are dried *round* noodles made from rice flour and look similar to bean threads.

Rice wine: low alcohol wine made from fermented rice. It is often used in Japanese cooking to add flavor to sauces and glazes but is also served as a beverage. It's available in Japanese markets and some supermarkets. If labeled as "cooking rice wine," it should be used only for cooking since it contains salt. Store in a cool, dark place. Dry sherry may be substituted in most recipes.

Satay (Saté) sauce (also called Chinese barbecue sauce): a dark brown, hot, spicy sauce composed of soy sauce, ground shrimp, chili peppers, sugar, garlic, oil and spices. It is available in cans or jars.

Sesame oil: an amber-colored oil pressed from toasted sesame seeds. It has a strong, nutlike flavor and is best used sparingly. Sesame oil is generally used as a flavoring, not as a cooking oil, because of its low smoking point. It is available in bottles.

Snow peas: (also called pea pods or Chinese peas): flat, green pods that are picked before the peas have matured. They add crispness, color and flavor to foods, require very little cooking and are frequently used in stir-fried dishes. Snow peas are available fresh or frozen.

Soy sauce: a pungent, brown, salty liquid made of fermented soybeans, wheat, yeast, salt and, sometimes, sugar. It is an essential ingredient in Chinese cooking. There are several types of soy sauces (light, dark, heavy), as well as Japanese-style soy sauce. The Japanese-style sauce is somewhere between light and dark varieties. All types of soy sauce are available in bottles.

Szechuan (Sichuan) peppercorns: a reddish-brown pepper with a strong, pungent aroma and flavor with a time-delayed action—its potent flavor may not be noticed immediately. It should be used sparingly. It is usually sold whole or crushed in small packages.

Vinegar, rice: a light, mellow and mildly tangy vinegar brewed from rice. Do not use brands that are not brewed or that are seasoned with salt and sugar. Cider vinegar can be used as a substitution for rice vinegar, except when preparing sushi rice. Store in a cool, dark place.

Water chestnut: a walnut-sized bulb from an aquatic plant. The bulb has a tough, brown skin and crisp white interior. Water chestnuts are served separately as a vegetable and are used to add crisp texture and delicate sweet flavor to dishes. They are available fresh or in cans.

Wonton wrappers: commercially prepared dough that is rolled thinly and cut into 3- to 4-inch squares. They are available fresh or frozen.

Wood ears (also called tree ears or cloud ears): a dried fungus that expands to five or six times its dehydrated size when soaked in warm water. They have a delicate flavor and crunchy texture and are most often used in soups. They are available in cellophane packages.

Shrimp Toast

12 **large shrimp, shelled and**
   deveined, leaving tails intact
1 **egg**
2½ **tablespoons cornstarch**
¼ **teaspoon salt**
   Dash of pepper
3 **slices white sandwich bread,**
   crusts removed and quartered
1 **slice cooked ham, cut into**
   ½-inch pieces
1 **hard-cooked egg yolk, cut into**
   ½-inch pieces
1 **green onion with top, finely**
   chopped
   Vegetable oil for frying
   Hard-cooked egg half and
   Green Onion Curls (page 170)
   for garnish

1. Cut deep slit down back of each shrimp; press gently with fingers to flatten.

2. Beat raw egg, cornstarch, salt and pepper in large bowl until blended. Add shrimp; toss to coat well.

3. Place one shrimp, cut-side down, on each bread piece; press shrimp gently into bread.

4. Brush small amount of egg mixture over each shrimp.

5. Place one piece *each* of ham and egg yolk and a scant ¼ teaspoon onion on top of each shrimp.

6. Heat oil in wok or large skillet over medium-high heat to 375°F. Add three or four bread pieces at a time; cook until golden, 1 to 2 minutes on each side. Drain on paper towels. Garnish, if desired.   *Makes 1 dozen*

Step 1. Flattening shrimp.

Step 4. Brushing egg mixture over shrimp.

Step 5. Placing egg yolk on shrimp.

Pot Stickers

2 cups all-purpose flour
³/₄ cup *plus* 2 tablespoons boiling
   water
¹/₂ cup very finely chopped napa
   cabbage
8 ounces lean ground pork
1 green onion with top, finely
   chopped
2 tablespoons finely chopped
   water chestnuts
1¹/₂ teaspoons soy sauce
1¹/₂ teaspoons dry sherry
1¹/₂ teaspoons cornstarch
¹/₂ teaspoon minced fresh ginger
¹/₂ teaspoon sesame oil
¹/₄ teaspoon sugar
2 tablespoons vegetable oil,
   divided
²/₃ cup chicken broth, divided
   Soy sauce, vinegar and chili oil

1. Place flour in large bowl; make well in center. Pour in boiling water; stir with wooden spoon until mixture forms dough.

2. Place dough on lightly floured surface; flatten slightly. To knead dough, fold dough in half toward you and press dough away from you with heel of hand. Give dough a quarter turn and continue folding, pushing and turning. Continue kneading 5 minutes or until smooth and elastic, adding additional flour to prevent sticking if necessary. Wrap dough in plastic wrap; let stand 30 minutes.

3. For filling, squeeze cabbage to remove as much moisture as possible; place in large bowl. Add pork, onion, water chestnuts, soy sauce, sherry, cornstarch, ginger, sesame oil and sugar; mix well.

4. Unwrap dough and knead briefly (as described in step 2) on lightly floured surface; divide into two equal pieces. Cover one piece with plastic wrap or clean towel while working with other piece.

5. Using lightly floured rolling pin, roll out dough to ¹/₈-inch thickness on lightly floured surface.

6. Cut out 3-inch circles with round cookie cutter or top of clean empty can.

7. Place 1 rounded teaspoon filling in center of each dough circle.

continued on page 166

Step 1. Stirring flour mixture to form dough.

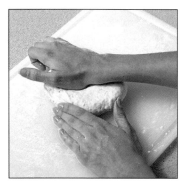

Step 2. Kneading dough.

Step 6. Cutting out dough circles.

Pot Stickers, continued

8. To shape each pot sticker, lightly moisten edge of one dough circle with water; fold in half.

9. Starting at one end, pinch curled edges together making four pleats along edge; set pot sticker down firmly, seam-side up. Cover finished pot stickers with plastic wrap while shaping remaining pot stickers.

10. Pot stickers may be cooked immediately or covered securely and stored in refrigerator up to 4 hours. Pot stickers may also be frozen. To freeze, place pot stickers on cookie sheet or shallow pan; place in freezer 30 minutes to firm slightly. Remove from freezer; place in freezer-weight resealable plastic bag. Freeze up to 3 months. (Frozen pot stickers do not need to be thawed before cooking.)

11. To cook pot stickers, heat 1 tablespoon vegetable oil in large nonstick skillet over medium heat. Place ¹/₂ of pot stickers in skillet, seam-side up. Cook until bottoms are golden brown, 5 to 6 minutes.

12. Pour in ¹/₃ cup chicken broth; cover tightly. Reduce heat to low. Simmer until all liquid is absorbed, about 10 minutes (15 minutes if frozen). Repeat with remaining vegetable oil, pot stickers and chicken broth.

13. Place pot stickers on serving platter. Serve with soy sauce, vinegar and chili oil for dipping.

Makes about 3 dozen

Step 8. Shaping pot stickers.

Step 9. Pleating pot stickers.

Step 11. Browning pot stickers.

Hors d'Oeuvre Rolls

**Sweet and Sour Sauce (recipe
  follows on page 168), optional
8 ounces deveined shelled shrimp
  (page 210)
1 package (17¼ ounces) frozen
  ready-to-bake puff pastry
  sheets *or* 40 wonton wrappers
½ cup Chinese-style thin egg
  noodles, broken into 1-inch
  pieces
2 tablespoons butter or
  margarine
4 ounces boneless lean pork,
  finely chopped
6 fresh medium mushrooms,
  finely chopped
6 green onions with tops, finely
  chopped
1 hard-cooked egg, finely
  chopped
1½ tablespoons dry sherry
½ teaspoon salt
⅛ teaspoon pepper
1 egg, lightly beaten
  Vegetable oil for frying
  Vegetable bundle* for garnish**

*To make vegetable bundle, cut 6- to 8-
inch length off top of green onion. Place
in salted water; let stand at least 15
minutes. Tie around small bundle of fresh
vegetables.

1. Prepare Sweet and Sour Sauce.

2. Place enough water to cover shrimp in
medium saucepan. Bring to a boil over
medium-high heat. Add shrimp. Reduce heat
to low. Simmer 5 to 10 minutes or until
shrimp curl and turn pink. (Do not overcook
shrimp as they will become tough.) Drain and
set aside to cool.

3. Remove puff pastry from freezer. Let stand,
uncovered, at room temperature until ready to
use, about 20 minutes.

4. Meanwhile, cook noodles according to
package directions just until tender but still
firm, 2 to 3 minutes. Drain and rinse under
cold running water; drain again. Chop
noodles finely.

5. Heat butter in wok or large skillet over
medium-high heat. Add pork; stir-fry until no
longer pink in center, about 5 minutes.

6. Add mushrooms and onions; stir-fry 2
minutes.

7. Remove wok from heat. Finely chop
shrimp. Add to wok with noodles, hard-
cooked egg, sherry, salt and pepper; mix well.

8. If using puff pastry, gently unfold each
pastry sheet. If pastry is too soft, place it in
refrigerator for a few minutes to chill. For ease
in handling, pastry should be cold to the
touch. Place pastry on lightly floured surface.
With lightly floured rolling pin, roll and trim
each sheet to 15 × 12-inch rectangle; cut into
twenty (3-inch) squares.

continued on page 168

Step 4. Chopping noodles.

Step 5. Stir-frying pork.

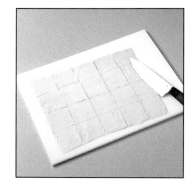

Step 8. Cutting out dough
squares.

Hors d'Oeurve Rolls, *continued*

9. Spoon 1 tablespoon pork mixture across center of each pastry square or wonton wrapper.

10. Brush edges lightly with beaten egg. Roll up tightly around filling; pinch edges slightly to seal.

11. Heat oil in wok or large skillet to 375°F. Add four to six rolls at a time; cook until golden and crisp, 3 to 5 minutes. Drain on paper towels. Garnish, if desired. Serve with Sweet and Sour Sauce. *Makes 40 rolls*

Sweet and Sour Sauce

4 teaspoons cornstarch
1 cup water
¹/₂ cup distilled white vinegar
¹/₂ cup sugar
¹/₄ cup tomato paste

Combine all ingredients in small saucepan. Bring to a boil over medium heat, stirring constantly. Boil 1 minute, stirring constantly. Set aside until ready to use or cover and refrigerate up to 8 hours.

Step 9. Spooning filling onto dough.

Step 10. Rolling up dough.

Step 11. Cooking rolls.

Barbecued Pork

¹/₄ cup soy sauce
2 tablespoons dry red wine
1 tablespoon packed brown sugar
1 tablespoon honey
2 teaspoons red food coloring
    (optional)
¹/₂ teaspoon ground cinnamon
1 green onion with top, cut in half
1 clove garlic, minced
2 whole pork tenderloins (about
    12 ounces each), trimmed
    Green Onion Curls (recipe
    follows) for garnish

1. Combine soy sauce, wine, sugar, honey, food coloring, cinnamon, onion and garlic in large bowl. Add meat; turn to coat completely. Cover and refrigerate 1 hour or overnight, turning meat occasionally.

2. Preheat oven to 350°F. Drain meat, reserving marinade. Place meat on wire rack over baking pan. Bake 45 minutes or until no longer pink in center, turning and basting frequently with reserved marinade.

3. Remove meat from oven; cool. Cut into diagonal slices. Garnish with Green Onion Curls, if desired.

Makes about 8 appetizer servings

Green Onion Curls

6 to 8 medium green onions with tops
    Cold water
10 to 12 ice cubes

1. Trim bulbs (white part) from onions; reserve for another use. Trim remaining stems (green part) to 4-inch lengths.

2. Using sharp scissors, cut each section of green stems lengthwise into very thin strips down to beginning of stems, cutting six to eight strips in each stem section.

3. Fill large bowl about half full with cold water. Add green onions and ice cubes. Refrigerate until onions curl, about 1 hour; drain.   *Makes 6 to 8 curls*

Green Onion Curls: Step 1.
Trimming onions.

Green Onion Curls: Step 2.
Cutting onion stems into strips.

Green Onion Curls: Step 3.
Soaking onions.

Long Soup

¹/₄ **of small head of cabbage**
   (4 to 6 ounces)
1¹/₂ **tablespoons vegetable oil**
   8 ounces boneless lean pork, cut
   into thin strips
   6 cups chicken broth
   2 tablespoons soy sauce
¹/₂ **teaspoon minced fresh ginger**
   8 green onions with tops,
   diagonally cut into ¹/₂-inch
   slices
   4 ounces Chinese-style thin egg
   noodles

1. Remove core from cabbage; discard.

2. Shred cabbage.

3. Heat oil in wok or large skillet over medium-high heat. Add cabbage and pork; stir-fry until pork is no longer pink in center, about 5 minutes.

4. Add chicken broth, soy sauce and ginger. Bring to a boil. Reduce heat to low; simmer 10 minutes, stirring occasionally. Stir in onions.

5. Add noodles.

6. Cook just until noodles are tender, 2 to 4 minutes.

Makes 4 servings

Step 1. Removing core from cabbage.

Step 5. Adding noodles to wok.

Step 6. Cooking noodles.

Wonton Soup

½ cup finely chopped cabbage
8 ounces lean ground pork
4 ounces deveined shelled shrimp, finely chopped
3 green onions with tops, finely chopped
1 egg, lightly beaten
1½ tablespoons cornstarch
2 teaspoons soy sauce
2 teaspoons sesame oil, divided
1 teaspoon oyster sauce
48 wonton wrappers (about 1 pound)
1 egg white, lightly beaten
¾ pound bok choy *or* napa cabbage
6 cups chicken broth
1 cup thinly sliced Barbecued Pork (page 170)
3 green onions with tops, thinly sliced
Edible flowers for garnish

1. For filling, squeeze cabbage to remove as much moisture as possible. Place cabbage in large bowl. Add pork, shrimp, chopped onions, whole egg, cornstarch, soy sauce, 1½ teaspoons sesame oil and oyster sauce; mix well.

2. For wontons, work with about twelve wrappers at a time, keeping remaining wrappers covered with plastic wrap. Place one wonton wrapper on work surface with one point facing you. Place 1 teaspoon filling in bottom corner; fold bottom corner over filling.

3. Moisten side corners of wonton wrapper with egg white. Bring side corners together, overlapping slightly; pinch together firmly to seal. Cover finished wontons with plastic wrap while filling remaining wontons. (Cook immediately, refrigerate up to 8 hours or freeze in resealable plastic bag.)

4. Add wontons to large pot of boiling water; cook until filling is no longer pink, about 4 minutes (6 minutes if frozen); drain. Place in bowl of cold water to prevent wontons from sticking together.

5. Cut bok choy stems into 1-inch slices; cut leaves in half crosswise. Set aside.

6. Bring chicken broth to a boil in large saucepan. Add bok choy and remaining ½ teaspoon sesame oil; simmer 2 minutes. Drain wontons; add to hot broth. Add slices of Barbecued Pork and sliced onions. Ladle into soup bowls. Serve immediately. Garnish, if desired. *Makes 6 servings*

Step 2. Folding wonton wrapper over filling.

Step 3. Shaping wontons.

Beef with Cashews

1 piece fresh ginger (about 1 inch
    square)
1 pound beef rump steak
4 tablespoons vegetable oil,
    divided
4 teaspoons cornstarch
1/2 cup water
4 teaspoons soy sauce
1 teaspoon sesame oil
1 teaspoon oyster sauce
1 teaspoon Chinese chili sauce
8 green onions with tops, cut into
    1-inch pieces
2 cloves garlic, minced
2/3 cup unsalted roasted cashews
    (about 3 ounces)
  Fresh carrot slices and thyme
    leaves for garnish

1. Peel and finely chop ginger; set aside.

2. Trim fat from meat; discard. Cut meat across grain into thin slices, each about 2 inches long.

3. Heat 1 tablespoon vegetable oil in wok or large skillet over high heat. Add 1/2 of meat; stir-fry until browned, 3 to 5 minutes. Remove from wok; set aside. Repeat with 1 tablespoon oil and remaining meat.

4. Combine cornstarch, water, soy sauce, sesame oil, oyster sauce and chili sauce in small bowl; mix well.

5. Heat remaining 2 tablespoons vegetable oil in wok or large skillet over high heat. Add ginger, onions, garlic and cashews; stir-fry 1 minute.

6. Stir cornstarch mixture; add to wok with meat. Cook and stir until liquid boils and thickens. Garnish, if desired.

Makes 4 servings

Step 1. Chopping peeled ginger.

Step 2. Cutting meat.

Step 5. Adding cashews to wok.

Mongolian Lamb

Sesame Sauce
  1 tablespoon sesame seeds
  ¼ cup soy sauce
  1 tablespoon dry sherry
  1 tablespoon red wine vinegar
  1½ teaspoons sugar
  1 clove garlic, minced
  1 green onion with top, finely
    chopped
  ½ teaspoon sesame oil

Lamb
  1 pound boneless lean lamb*
    (leg or shoulder)
  2 small leeks
  4 green onions with tops
  2 medium carrots, shredded
  1 medium zucchini, shredded
  1 *each* green and red pepper, cut
    into matchstick pieces
  ½ small head napa cabbage, thinly
    sliced
  1 cup bean sprouts
  4 tablespoons vegetable oil,
    divided
  4 slices peeled fresh ginger
    Chili oil (optional)

*Or, substitute beef flank steak or
boneless lean pork for the lamb.

1. For Sesame Sauce, place sesame seeds in small skillet. Carefully shake or stir over medium heat until seeds begin to pop and turn golden brown, about 2 minutes; cool.

2. Crush seeds with mortar and pestle (or place between paper towels and crush with rolling pin); scrape up sesame paste with knife and transfer to small serving bowl. Add remaining sauce ingredients; mix well.

3. Slice meat across grain into 2 × ¼-inch strips.

4. Cut leek into 2-inch slivers. Repeat with green onions.

5. Arrange meat and all vegetables on large platter. Have Sesame Sauce, vegetable oil, ginger and chili oil near cooking area.

6. Heat wok or electric griddle to 350°F. Cook one serving at a time. For each serving, heat 1 tablespoon vegetable oil. Add one slice ginger; cook and stir 30 seconds. Discard ginger. Add ½ cup meat strips; stir-fry until lightly browned, about 1 minute. Add 2 cups assorted vegetables; stir-fry 1 minute. Drizzle with 2 tablespoons Sesame Sauce; stir-fry 30 seconds. Season with a few drops chili oil. Repeat with remaining ingredients.

Makes 4 servings

Step 4. Cutting leek.

Step 5. Arranging cut-up ingredients on platter.

Two-Onion Pork Shreds

¹/₂ teaspoon Szechuan
   peppercorns*
1 teaspoon cornstarch
4 teaspoons soy sauce, divided
4 teaspoons dry sherry, divided
7¹/₂ teaspoons vegetable oil, divided
8 ounces boneless lean pork
2 teaspoons red wine vinegar
¹/₂ teaspoon sugar
2 cloves garlic, minced
¹/₂ small yellow onion, cut into
   ¹/₄-inch slices
8 green onions with tops, cut into
   2-inch pieces
¹/₂ teaspoon sesame oil

*Szechuan peppercorns are deceptively
potent. Wear rubber or plastic gloves
when crushing them and do not touch
your eyes or lips when handling.

1. For marinade, place peppercorns in small skillet. Cook over medium-low heat, shaking skillet frequently, until fragrant, about 2 minutes. Let cool.

2. Crush peppercorns with mortar and pestle (or place between paper towels and crush with hammer).

3. Transfer peppercorns to medium bowl. Add cornstarch, 2 teaspoons soy sauce, 2 teaspoons sherry and 1¹/₂ teaspoons vegetable oil; mix well.

4. Slice meat ¹/₈ inch thick; cut into 2 × ¹/₂-inch pieces. Add to marinade; stir to coat well. Cover and refrigerate 30 minutes, stirring occasionally.

5. Combine remaining 2 teaspoons soy sauce, 2 teaspoons sherry, vinegar and sugar in small bowl; mix well.

6. Heat remaining 6 teaspoons vegetable oil in wok or large skillet over high heat. Stir in garlic. Add meat mixture; stir-fry until no longer pink in center, about 2 minutes. Add yellow onion; stir-fry 1 minute. Add green onions; stir-fry 30 seconds.

7. Add soy-vinegar mixture; cook and stir 30 seconds. Stir in sesame oil.

Makes 2 to 3 servings

Step 2. Crushing peppercorns.

Step 4. Adding meat to marinade.

Step 6. Adding green onions to wok.

Honey-Glazed Spareribs

1 side pork spareribs (about 2 pounds)
¼ cup *plus* 1 tablespoon soy sauce, divided
3 tablespoons hoisin sauce
3 tablespoons dry sherry, divided
1 tablespoon sugar
1 teaspoon minced fresh ginger
2 cloves garlic, minced
¼ teaspoon Chinese five-spice powder
2 tablespoons honey
1 tablespoon cider vinegar
Green Onion Curls (page 170), slivered green onions and edible flowers for garnish

1. Have your butcher cut ribs down length of slab into two pieces so that each half is 2 to 3 inches wide. Cut between bones to make 6-inch pieces.

2. Trim excess fat from ribs. Place ribs in heavy resealable plastic bag.

3. For marinade, combine ¼ cup soy sauce, hoisin sauce, 2 tablespoons sherry, sugar, ginger, garlic and five-spice powder in small cup or bowl; mix well. Pour over ribs.

4. Seal bag tightly; place in large bowl. Refrigerate at least 8 hours or overnight, turning bag occasionally.

5. Preheat oven to 350°F. Line large baking pan with foil. Place ribs on rack in pan, reserving marinade. Bake 30 minutes; turn ribs over. Brush with marinade; continue baking 40 minutes or until ribs are tender when pierced with fork.

6. For glaze, combine honey, vinegar, remaining 1 tablespoon soy sauce and 1 tablespoon sherry in small bowl; mix well. Brush ½ of mixture over ribs. Place under broiler 4 to 6 inches from heat source; broil until glaze is hot and bubbly, 2 to 3 minutes. Turn ribs over. Brush with remaining honey glaze.

7. Broil until hot and bubbly. Cut into serving-size pieces. Garnish, if desired.

Makes about 4 servings

Step 1. Cutting ribs into 6-inch pieces.

Step 3. Pouring marinade over ribs.

Step 6. Brushing ribs with glaze.

Sweet and Sour Pork

1 egg yolk, lightly beaten
$\frac{1}{4}$ cup soy sauce
1$\frac{1}{2}$ tablespoons dry sherry
2 teaspoons sugar
2 pounds boneless lean pork, cut into 1-inch pieces
$\frac{1}{2}$ cup *plus* 2 tablespoons cornstarch, divided
1 can (20 ounces) pineapple chunks in syrup, undrained
$\frac{1}{4}$ cup rice vinegar
3 tablespoons tomato sauce
1 cup water
1 medium cucumber
3 cups *plus* 3 tablespoons vegetable oil, divided
1 large yellow onion, thinly sliced
8 green onions with tops, diagonally cut into 1-inch pieces
1 red or green pepper, chopped
4 ounces fresh mushrooms, cut into quarters
2 stalks celery, diagonally cut into $\frac{1}{2}$-inch slices
Celery leaves and red pepper curls* for garnish

*To make red pepper curls, cut additional red pepper into thin strips. Add to small bowl of salted water. Let stand until slightly softened, 1 to 2 hours. Wrap pepper strips around finger to curl.

1. For marinade, combine egg yolk, soy sauce, sherry and sugar in large bowl. Add meat; stir to coat well. Cover and refrigerate 1 hour, stirring occasionally.

2. Drain meat, reserving marinade. Place $\frac{1}{2}$ cup cornstarch in large bowl. Add meat; toss to coat well. Set aside.

3. Drain pineapple, reserving syrup. Add syrup to reserved marinade with vinegar and tomato sauce; stir until well blended. Set aside. Combine remaining 2 tablespoons cornstarch and water in another small bowl; mix well. Set aside.

4. Cut cucumber in half lengthwise; remove seeds.

5. Cut cucumber into $\frac{1}{4}$-inch pieces; set aside.

6. Heat 3 cups oil in wok or large skillet over high heat to 375°F. Add $\frac{1}{2}$ of meat. Cook until no longer pink in center, about 5 minutes; drain on paper towels. Repeat with remaining meat.

7. Heat remaining 3 tablespoons oil in wok over high heat. Add vegetables; stir-fry 3 minutes. Stir cornstarch mixture. Add to wok with pineapple syrup mixture; cook and stir until sauce boils and thickens. Add meat and pineapple; stir-fry until thoroughly heated. Garnish, if desired. *Makes 4 servings*

Step 2. Coating pork with cornstarch.

Step 4. Removing cucumber seeds.

Vermicelli with Pork

4 ounces Chinese rice vermicelli
  or **bean threads**
32 **dried mushrooms**
  1 **small red** *or* **green hot chili**
    pepper*
  3 **green onions with tops, divided**
  2 **tablespoons minced fresh ginger**
  2 **tablespoons hot bean sauce**
1½ **cups chicken broth**
  1 **tablespoon soy sauce**
  1 **tablespoon dry sherry**
  2 **tablespoons vegetable oil**
  6 **ounces lean ground pork**
    Fresh cilantro leaves and hot
      red pepper for garnish

*Hot chili peppers are deceptively potent.
Wear rubber or plastic gloves when
removing seeds or chopping peppers and
do not touch your eyes or lips when
handling.

1. Place vermicelli and dried mushrooms in separate large bowls; cover each with hot water. Let stand 30 minutes; drain. Cut vermicelli into 4-inch pieces.

2. Squeeze out as much excess water as possible from mushrooms. Cut off and discard mushroom stems; cut caps into thin slices.

3. Cut chili pepper in half; scrape out seeds.

4. Finely chop chili pepper.

5. Cut one onion into 1½-inch slivers; reserve for garnish. Cut remaining two onions into thin slices.

6. Combine ginger and hot bean sauce in small bowl; set aside. Combine chicken broth, soy sauce and sherry in another small bowl; set aside.

7. Heat oil in wok or large skillet over high heat. Add meat; stir-fry until no longer pink, about 2 minutes. Add chili pepper, sliced onions and bean sauce mixture; stir-fry 1 minute.

8. Add chicken broth mixture, vermicelli and mushrooms. Simmer, uncovered, until most of the liquid is absorbed, about 5 minutes. Top with onion slivers. Garnish, if desired.

Makes 4 servings

Step 1. Cutting vermicelli.

Step 2. Slicing mushrooms.

Step 3. Removing pepper seeds.

Mu Shu Pork

4 teaspoons cornstarch, divided
8 teaspoons soy sauce, divided
5 teaspoons dry sherry, divided
8 ounces boneless lean pork, cut
   into matchstick pieces
3 dried mushrooms
2 dried wood ears
   Water
½ teaspoon sugar
1 teaspoon sesame oil
2 tablespoons *plus* 1 teaspoon
   vegetable oil, divided
2 eggs, lightly beaten
1 teaspoon minced fresh ginger
½ cup sliced bamboo shoots
   (½ of 8-ounce can), cut into
   matchstick pieces
1 small carrot, shredded
½ cup chicken broth
2 cups bean sprouts (about
   4 ounces)
2 green onions with tops, cut into
   1½-inch slivers
½ cup hoisin sauce
16 Mandarin Pancakes (recipe
   follows on page 194)

1. For marinade, combine 1 teaspoon cornstarch, 2 teaspoons soy sauce and 2 teaspoons sherry in large bowl. Add meat; stir to coat. Let stand 30 minutes.

2. Meanwhile, place dried mushrooms and wood ears in small bowl; add enough water to cover. Let stand 30 minutes; drain. Squeeze out excess water. Cut off and discard mushroom stems; cut caps into thin slices.

3. Pinch out hard nobs from center of wood ears; discard.

4. Cut wood ears into thin strips.

5. Combine remaining 3 teaspoons cornstarch, 6 teaspoons soy sauce and 3 teaspoons sherry in small bowl. Add additional 1 tablespoon water, sugar and sesame oil; mix well.

6. Heat ½ teaspoon vegetable oil in small nonstick skillet over medium-high heat. Add ½ of eggs, tilting skillet to cover bottom.

7. Cook eggs just until set. Loosen edges and turn omelet over; cook 5 seconds.

8. Remove omelet from skillet; set aside to cool. Repeat with another ½ teaspoon vegetable oil and remaining eggs.

9. Cut omelets in half. Stack halves; cut crosswise into thin strips.

10. Heat remaining 2 tablespoons vegetable oil in wok or large skillet over high heat. Stir in ginger. Add meat; stir-fry until meat is no longer pink in center, about 2 minutes. Add mushrooms, wood ears, bamboo shoots, carrot and chicken broth; stir-fry 2 minutes.

Step 3. Removing nobs from wood ears.

Step 6. Tilting skillet to cover bottom with eggs.

Step 7. Loosening omelet from skillet.

continued on page 194

Mu Shu Pork, continued

11. Add bean sprouts and onions; stir-fry 1 minute.

12. Stir cornstarch mixture; add to wok. Cook, stirring constantly, until sauce bubbles and thickens. Stir in omelet strips.

13. To serve, spread about 2 teaspoons hoisin sauce onto each pancake. Spoon about 3 tablespoons pork mixture down center. Fold over bottom; roll up.

Makes 8 servings

Mandarin Pancakes

2 cups all-purpose flour
³/4 cup boiling water
2 tablespoons sesame oil

1. Place flour in bowl; make well in center. Pour in boiling water.

2. Stir flour mixture with wooden spoon until dough looks like lumpy meal.

3. Press dough into ball. On lightly floured surface, knead dough until smooth and satiny, about 5 minutes (page 164). Cover with clean towel and let rest 30 minutes.

4. Roll dough into log, 10 inches long. Cut into 1-inch pieces; cover with plastic wrap.

5. Cut each piece of dough in half, keeping remaining dough pieces covered with plastic wrap. Shape each half into ball. Place on lightly floured surface; flatten slightly. With lightly floured rolling pin, roll each dough piece into 3-inch circle; brush with small amount of sesame oil. Stack two dough circles together, oil-side in.

6. Roll each pair of dough circles into 6- to 7-inch circle; cover and set aside. Repeat with remaining dough circles.

7. Heat nonstick skillet over medium-low heat. Cook pancakes, one pair at a time, turning every 30 seconds, until cakes are flecked with brown and feel dry, 2 to 3 minutes. (Be careful not to overcook pancakes or they will become brittle.)

8. Remove pancakes from pan. Separate each pancake into two pancakes while still hot. Stack pancakes on plate; keep covered while cooking remaining pancakes. Fold pancakes into quarters and arrange in serving basket. Serve immediately.

Makes about 20 pancakes

Note: Pancakes may be prepared ahead and refrigerated or frozen in resealable plastic bags.

To reheat, wrap pancakes in clean towel (thaw completely, if using frozen). Steam over simmering water 5 minutes.

Mandarin Pancakes: Step 2. Stirring flour mixture to form dough.

Mandarin Pancakes: Step 6. Rolling out dough circles.

Mandarin Pancakes: Step 7. Cooking pancakes.

How to Cut Chicken Chinese-Style

Recipes for Chinese chicken dishes often instruct that chicken be cut into serving-size pieces. These pieces should be smaller than chicken pieces generally are cut. Following are directions for cutting a whole chicken Chinese-style. A cleaver is the best utensil for chopping a chicken, although poultry shears or a sharp knife may also be used.

1. Place chicken, breast-side up, on heavy cutting board. Cut in half lengthwise, cutting slightly to one side of breastbone and backbone. (Cut completely through chicken to make two pieces.)

2. Remove and discard backbone, if desired.

3. Pull each leg up slightly from breast section; cut through ball and socket joint to remove each leg. Cut through knee joint of each leg to separate into drumstick and thigh.

4. Pull each wing away from breast; cut through joint next to breast.

5. Cut each drumstick, thigh and breast piece crosswise into three pieces, cutting completely through bones. Cut each wing into two pieces.

Makes 22 small serving-size pieces

Step 1. Cutting chicken in half.

Step 3. Cutting knee joint.

Step 4. Cutting wing joint.

Hoisin Chicken

1 broiler-fryer chicken (3 to 4 pounds)
1/2 cup *plus* 1 tablespoon cornstarch, divided
1 cup water
3 tablespoons dry sherry
3 tablespoons cider vinegar
3 tablespoons hoisin sauce
4 teaspoons soy sauce
2 teaspoons instant chicken bouillon granules
Vegetable oil for frying
2 teaspoons minced fresh ginger
2 medium onions, chopped
8 ounces fresh broccoli, cut into 1-inch pieces
1 red or green pepper, chopped
2 cans (4 ounces each) whole button mushrooms, drained
Vermicelli (page 235), optional
Additional red pepper, cut into matchstick pieces, for garnish

1. Rinse chicken; cut Chinese-style (page 195).

2. Combine 1 tablespoon cornstarch, water, sherry, vinegar, hoisin sauce, soy sauce and bouillon granules in small bowl; mix well. Set aside.

3. Place remaining 1/2 cup cornstarch in large bowl. Add chicken pieces; stir to coat well.

4. Heat oil in large skillet or wok over high heat to 375°F. Add 1/3 of the chicken pieces, one at a time; cook until no longer pink in center, about 5 minutes. Drain chicken pieces on paper towels. Repeat with remaining chicken.

5. Remove all but 2 tablespoons oil from skillet. Add ginger to skillet; stir-fry 1 minute. Add onions; stir-fry 1 minute. Add broccoli, pepper and mushrooms; stir-fry 2 minutes.

6. Stir cornstarch mixture; add to skillet. Cook and stir until sauce boils and thickens.

7. Return chicken to skillet. Cook and stir until chicken is thoroughly heated, about 2 minutes. Serve over hot Vermicelli and garnish, if desired.   *Makes 6 servings*

Step 1. Cutting chicken Chinese-style.

Step 4. Cooking chicken.

Kung Pao Chicken

3¹/₂ **teaspoons cornstarch, divided**
  5 **teaspoons soy sauce, divided**
  5 **teaspoons dry sherry, divided**
  ¹/₄ **teaspoon salt**
  3 **boneless skinless chicken breast**
    halves, cut into bite-size pieces
  1 **tablespoon red wine vinegar**
  2 **tablespoons chicken broth** *or*
    water
1¹/₂ **teaspoons sugar**
  3 **tablespoons vegetable oil,**
    divided
  ¹/₃ **cup salted peanuts**
  6 **to 8 small dried hot chili**
    peppers
1¹/₂ **teaspoons minced fresh ginger**
  2 **green onions with tops, cut into**
    1¹/₂-**inch pieces**
    Additional green onion and
    dried hot chili pepper for
    garnish

1. For marinade, combine 2 teaspoons cornstarch, 2 teaspoons soy sauce, 2 teaspoons sherry and salt in large bowl; mix well. Add chicken; stir to coat well. Let stand 30 minutes.

2. Combine remaining 1¹/₂ teaspoons cornstarch, 3 teaspoons soy sauce, 3 teaspoons sherry, vinegar, chicken broth and sugar in small bowl; mix well. Set aside.

3. Heat 1 tablespoon oil in wok or large skillet over medium heat. Add peanuts; cook and stir until lightly toasted. Remove peanuts from wok; set aside.

4. Heat remaining 2 tablespoons oil in wok over medium heat. Add chili peppers; stir-fry until peppers just begin to char, about 1 minute.

5. Increase heat to high. Add chicken mixture; stir-fry 2 minutes. Add ginger; stir-fry until chicken is no longer pink in center, about 1 minute.

6. Add peanuts and onions; stir-fry 1 minute.

7. Stir cornstarch mixture; add to wok. Cook and stir until sauce boils and thickens. Garnish, if desired.   *Makes 3 servings*

Step 3. Toasting peanuts.

Step 4. Stir-frying chili peppers.

Step 6. Stir-frying peanuts and onions with chicken mixture.

Chicken Chow Mein

Fried Noodles (page 234)
2 whole chicken breasts
8 ounces boneless lean pork
3 teaspoons cornstarch, divided
2 tablespoons *plus* **1½ teaspoons dry sherry**
1½ tablespoons *plus* **1½ teaspoons soy sauce**
½ cup water
2 teaspoons instant chicken bouillon granules
2 tablespoons vegetable oil
1 piece fresh ginger (1-inch square), peeled and finely chopped
1 clove garlic, minced
8 ounces deveined shelled shrimp (page 210)
2 medium yellow onions, chopped
1 red or green pepper, thinly sliced
2 stalks celery, diagonally cut into 1-inch slices
8 green onions with tops, chopped
4 ounces cabbage (¼ of small head), shredded

1. Prepare Fried Noodles; set aside.

2. Remove skin and bones from chicken breasts.

3. Cut chicken and pork into 1-inch pieces.

4. Combine 1 teaspoon cornstarch, 1½ teaspoons sherry and 1½ teaspoons soy sauce in large bowl. Add chicken and pork; toss to coat well. Cover and refrigerate 1 hour.

5. Combine remaining 2 teaspoons cornstarch, 2 tablespoons sherry, 1½ tablespoons soy sauce, water and boullion granules in small bowl; set aside.

6. Heat oil in wok or large skillet over high heat. Add ginger and garlic; stir-fry 1 minute. Add chicken and pork; stir-fry until no longer pink in center, about 5 minutes. Add shrimp; stir-fry until shrimp turn pink, about 3 minutes.

7. Add vegetables to wok; stir-fry until crisp-tender, 3 to 5 minutes. Add bouillon-soy sauce mixture. Cook and stir until sauce boils and thickens; cook and stir an additional minute.

8. Arrange Fried Noodles on serving plate; top with chicken mixture.

Makes 6 servings

Step 2. Removing chicken bones.

Step 3. Cutting chicken and pork.

Step 6. Stir-frying shrimp with chicken mixture.

Asparagus Chicken with Black Bean Sauce

5 teaspoons cornstarch, divided
4 teaspoons soy sauce, divided
1 tablespoon dry sherry
1 teaspoon sesame oil
3 boneless skinless chicken breast
    halves, cut into bite-sized pieces
1 tablespoon fermented, salted
    black beans
1 teaspoon minced fresh ginger
1 clove garlic, minced
½ cup chicken broth
1 tablespoon oyster sauce
1 medium-size yellow onion
3 tablespoons vegetable oil,
    divided
1 pound fresh asparagus spears,
    trimmed and diagonally cut
    into 1-inch pieces
2 tablespoons water
    Fresh cilantro leaves for garnish

1. Combine 2 teaspoons cornstarch, 2 teaspoons soy sauce, sherry and sesame oil in large bowl; mix well. Add chicken; stir to coat well. Let stand 30 minutes.

2. Place beans in sieve; rinse under cold running water. Finely chop beans. Combine with ginger and garlic; set aside.

3. Combine remaining 3 teaspoons cornstarch, remaining 2 teaspoons soy sauce, chicken broth and oyster sauce in small bowl; mix well. Set aside.

4. Peel onion; cut into eight wedges. Separate wedges; set aside.

5. Heat 2 tablespoons vegetable oil in wok or large skillet over high heat. Add chicken mixture; stir-fry until chicken is no longer pink in center, about 3 minutes. Remove from wok; set aside.

6. Heat remaining 1 tablespoon vegetable oil in wok. Add onion and asparagus; stir-fry 30 seconds.

7. Add water; cover. Cook, stirring occasionally, until asparagus is crisp-tender, about 2 minutes. Return chicken to wok.

8. Stir chicken broth mixture; add to wok with bean mixture. Cook until sauce boils and thickens, stirring constantly. Garnish, if desired.   *Makes 3 to 4 servings*

Step 4. Separating onion wedges.

Step 6. Stir-frying onion and asparagus.

Chicken with Lychees

3 whole boneless skinless chicken breasts
¼ cup *plus* 1 teaspoon cornstarch, divided
½ cup water, divided
½ cup tomato sauce
1 teaspoon sugar
1 teaspoon instant chicken bouillon granules
3 tablespoons vegetable oil
1 red pepper, cut into 1-inch pieces
6 green onions with tops, cut into 1-inch pieces
1 can (11 ounces) whole peeled lychees, drained
Vermicelli (page 235), optional
Fresh cilantro leaves for garnish

1. Cut chicken breasts in half; cut each half into six pieces.

2. Place ¼ cup cornstarch in large resealable plastic bag. Add chicken pieces; close bag tightly. Shake bag until chicken is well coated; set aside.

3. Combine remaining 1 teaspoon cornstarch and ¼ cup water in small bowl; mix well. Set aside.

4. Combine remaining ¼ cup water, tomato sauce, sugar and bouillon granules in small bowl; mix well. Set aside.

5. Heat oil in wok or large skillet over high heat. Add chicken; stir-fry until lightly browned, 5 to 8 minutes. Add red pepper and onions; stir-fry 1 minute.

6. Pour tomato sauce mixture over chicken mixture. Stir in lychees.

7. Reduce heat to low; cover. Simmer until chicken is tender and no longer pink in center, about 5 minutes.

8. Stir cornstarch mixture; add to wok. Cook and stir until sauce boils and thickens. Serve over hot Vermicelli and garnish, if desired.

Makes 4 servings

Step 1. Cutting chicken.

Step 2. Coating chicken with cornstarch.

Step 6. Stirring lychees into other ingredients in wok.

Almond Chicken

2¹/₂ tablespoons cornstarch, divided
1¹/₂ cups water
    4 tablespoons dry sherry, divided
    4 teaspoons soy sauce
    1 teaspoon instant chicken
       bouillon granules
    1 egg white
¹/₂ teaspoon salt
    4 whole boneless skinless chicken
       breasts, cut into 1-inch pieces
    Vegetable oil for frying
¹/₂ cup blanched whole almonds
      (about 3 ounces)
    1 large carrot, finely chopped
    1 teaspoon minced fresh ginger
    6 green onions with tops, cut into
      1-inch pieces
    3 stalks celery, diagonally cut
      into ¹/₂-inch pieces
¹/₂ cup sliced bamboo shoots (¹/₂ of
      8-ounce can), drained
    8 fresh mushrooms, sliced
    Fried Noodles (page 234),
      optional
    Carrot strips and fresh cilantro
      leaves for garnish

1. Combine 1¹/₂ tablespoons cornstarch, water, 2 tablespoons sherry, soy sauce and bouillon granules in small saucepan. Cook and stir over medium heat until mixture boils and thickens, about 5 minutes; keep warm.

2. Beat egg white in medium bowl until foamy.

3. Add remaining 1 tablespoon cornstarch, 2 tablespoons sherry and salt to egg white; mix well. Add chicken pieces; stir to coat well.

4. Heat about 2 inches oil in wok or large skillet over high heat to 375°F. Add ¹/₃ of chicken pieces, two at a time; cook until no longer pink in center, 3 to 5 minutes. Drain chicken pieces on paper towels. Repeat with remaining chicken.

5. Remove all but 2 tablespoons oil from wok. Add almonds; stir-fry until golden brown, about 2 minutes. Remove almonds from wok; set aside.

6. Add carrot and ginger to wok; stir-fry 1 minute. Add onions, celery, bamboo shoots and mushrooms; stir-fry until celery is crisp-tender, about 3 minutes. Stir in chicken, almonds and cornstarch mixture; cook and stir until thoroughly heated. Serve with Fried Noodles and garnish, if desired.

Makes 4 to 6 servings

Step 1. Cooking sauce.

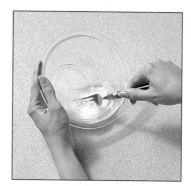
Step 2. Beating egg white.

Step 4. Cooking chicken.

Chinese Chicken Salad

2 whole chicken breasts
4 cups water
1 tablespoon dry sherry
2 slices peeled fresh ginger
5 green onions with tops, divided
¼ cup Chinese plum sauce
2 tablespoons rice vinegar
1 tablespoon vegetable oil
1 tablespoon sesame oil
1½ teaspoons soy sauce
4½ teaspoons sugar
1 teaspoon dry mustard
3 tablespoons slivered almonds
2 tablespoons sesame seeds
4 cups shredded iceberg lettuce
1 small carrot, shredded
1½ cups bean sprouts (about
    3 ounces)
¼ cup fresh cilantro leaves
    (Chinese parsley)
    Bean threads *or* Vermicelli
    (page 235), cooked and
    drained
    Additional fresh cilantro leaves
    and edible flowers for garnish

1. Combine chicken, water, sherry, ginger and two whole green onions in 3-quart saucepan. Bring to a boil over medium-high heat. Reduce heat to low; cover. Simmer 20 minutes or until chicken is no longer pink in center.

2. Remove saucepan from heat. Let stand until chicken is cool. Remove chicken from stock; set aside. Strain stock; refrigerate or freeze for another use.

3. Remove and discard skin and bones from chicken. Pull meat into long shreds; set aside.

4. For dressing, combine plum sauce, vinegar, vegetable and sesame oils, soy sauce, sugar and mustard in small bowl; mix well. Set aside.

5. Toast almonds by shaking in small dry skillet over medium heat until golden brown and fragrant, about 3 minutes. Place in large salad bowl. Toast sesame seeds in same skillet until seeds are golden brown and begin to pop, about 2 minutes. Add sesame seeds to almonds.

6. Cut remaining three green onions with tops into 1½-inch slivers.

7. Add onions to salad bowl with lettuce, carrot, bean sprouts, cilantro, chicken and dressing; toss to coat. Add bean threads; mix lightly. Garnish, if desired.

Makes 6 to 8 servings

Step 1. Cooking chicken.

Step 3. Shredding chicken.

Step 6. Cutting onions into slivers.

Braised Shrimp with Vegetables

1 teaspoon cornstarch
1/2 cup chicken broth
1 teaspoon oyster sauce
1/2 teaspoon minced fresh ginger
1/4 teaspoon sugar
1/8 teaspoon pepper
8 ounces fresh broccoli
1 pound large shrimp
1 tablespoon vegetable oil
2 cans (4 ounces each) whole
    button mushrooms, drained
1 can (8 ounces) sliced bamboo
    shoots, drained

1. Combine cornstarch, broth, oyster sauce, ginger, sugar and pepper in small bowl; mix well. Set aside.

2. Remove woody stems from broccoli; discard.

3. Coarsely chop head of broccoli and remaining stems; set aside.

4. Peel shells from shrimp. Remove veins with sharp knife.

5. Heat oil in wok or large skillet over high heat. Add shrimp; stir-fry until shrimp turn pink, about 3 minutes.

6. Add broccoli to wok; stir-fry 1 minute. Add mushrooms and bamboo shoots; stir-fry 1 minute.

7. Stir cornstarch mixture; add to wok. Cook and stir until sauce boils and thickens, about 2 minutes.   *Makes 4 servings*

Step 2. Removing broccoli stems.

Step 4. Deveining shrimp.

Step 5. Stir-frying shrimp.

Scallops with Vegetables

1 ounce dried mushrooms
  Water
4 teaspoons cornstarch
2½ tablespoons dry sherry
4 teaspoons soy sauce
2 teaspoons instant chicken
  bouillon granules
8 ounces fresh green beans
1 pound fresh *or* thawed frozen
  sea scallops
2 tablespoons vegetable oil
2 yellow onions, cut into 8 wedges
  and separated (page 202)
3 stalks celery, diagonally cut
  into ½-inch pieces
2 teaspoons minced fresh ginger
1 clove garlic, minced
6 green onions with tops,
  diagonally cut into thin slices
1 can (15 ounces) baby corn,
  drained
  Whole dried mushroom and
  celery leaves for garnish

1. Place mushrooms in bowl. Add enough water to cover; let stand 30 minutes. Drain. Squeeze out as much water as possible from mushrooms. Cut off and discard stems; cut caps into thin slices.

2. Combine cornstarch and additional 1 cup water in small bowl; stir in sherry, soy sauce and bouillon granules. Set aside.

3. Trim green beans; discard ends. Diagonally cut beans into 1-inch pieces.

4. Cut scallops into quarters; set aside.

5. Heat oil in wok or large skillet over high heat. Add green beans, yellow onions, celery, ginger and garlic; stir-fry 3 minutes.

6. Stir cornstarch mixture; add to wok. Cook and stir until sauce boils and thickens.

7. Add mushrooms, scallops, green onions and baby corn.

8. Cook and stir until scallops turn opaque, about 4 minutes. Garnish, if desired.

Makes 4 to 6 servings

Step 3. Trimming beans.

Step 4. Quartering scallops.

Step 7. Adding corn to wok.

Lo Mein Noodles with Shrimp

12 ounces Chinese-style thin egg
  noodles
2 teaspoons sesame oil
  Chinese chives*
1½ tablespoons oyster sauce
1½ tablespoons soy sauce
  ½ teaspoon sugar
  ¼ teaspoon salt
  ¼ teaspoon ground white *or* black
    pepper
2 tablespoons vegetable oil
1 teaspoon minced fresh ginger
1 clove garlic, minced
8 ounces medium shrimp, shelled
  and deveined (page 210)
1 tablespoon dry sherry
8 ounces bean sprouts

*Or, substitute ¼ cup domestic chives cut
into 1-inch pieces and 2 green onions with
tops, cut into 1-inch pieces, for the
Chinese chives.

1. Add noodles to boiling water; cook according to package directions until tender but still firm, 2 to 3 minutes.

2. Drain noodles; rinse under cold running water. Drain again.

3. Combine noodles and sesame oil in large bowl; toss lightly to coat.

4. Cut enough chives into 1-inch pieces to measure ½ cup; set aside.

5. Combine oyster sauce, soy sauce, sugar, salt and pepper in small bowl.

6. Heat vegetable oil in wok or large skillet over high heat. Add ginger and garlic; stir-fry 10 seconds. Add shrimp; stir-fry until shrimp begin to turn pink, about 1 minute. Add chives and sherry; stir-fry until chives begin to wilt, about 15 seconds. Add ½ of the bean sprouts; stir-fry 15 seconds. Add remaining bean sprouts; stir-fry 15 seconds.

7. Add oyster sauce mixture and noodles. Cook and stir until thoroughly heated, about 2 minutes. *Makes 4 servings*

Step 1. Adding noodles to boiling water.

Step 2. Rinsing cooked noodles.

Step 4. Snipping chives.

Fish Rolls with Crab Sauce

1 pound sole fillets, ¼- to ⅜-inch
  thick (about 4 ounces each)
2 tablespoons dry sherry
2 teaspoons sesame oil
1 green onion with top, finely
  chopped
1 teaspoon minced fresh ginger
½ teaspoon salt
  Dash of ground white pepper

Crab Sauce
1½ tablespoons cornstarch
2 tablespoons water
1 tablespoon vegetable oil
1 teaspoon minced fresh ginger
2 green onions with tops, thinly
  sliced
6 ounces fresh crabmeat, flaked
1¼ cups chicken broth
¼ cup milk

  Scored cucumber slices,* lemon
  wedges and fresh tarragon

*To score cucumber, run tines of fork
lengthwise down all sides of cucumber
before slicing.

1. If fillets are large, cut in half crosswise (each piece should be 5 to 6 inches long).

2. Combine 1 tablespoon sherry, sesame oil, chopped green onion, 1 teaspoon ginger, salt and white pepper in small bowl. Brush each piece of fish with sherry mixture; let stand 30 minutes.

3. Fold fish into thirds; place in rimmed heatproof dish that will fit inside a steamer.

4. Place dish on rack in steamer; cover steamer. Steam over boiling water until fish turns opaque and flakes easily with fork, 8 to 10 minutes. Meanwhile, combine cornstarch and water in small cup.

5. Heat vegetable oil in 2-quart saucepan over medium heat. Add 1 teaspoon ginger; cook and stir 10 seconds. Add sliced green onions, 1 remaining tablespoon sherry and crabmeat; stir-fry 1 minute. Add chicken broth and milk; bring to a boil. Stir cornstarch mixture; add to saucepan. Cook, stirring constantly, until sauce boils and thickens slightly.

6. Using slotted spoon, transfer fish to serving platter; top with Crab Sauce. Garnish, if desired.　　*Makes 4 to 6 servings*

Step 2. Brushing fish with sherry mixture.

Step 3. Placing fish in rimmed dish.

Step 4. Placing fish on rack in steamer.

Seafood Combination

Fried Noodles (page 234)
8 ounces fresh *or* thawed frozen
  shrimp
8 ounces fresh *or* thawed frozen
  fish fillets
2 teaspoons cornstarch
1/2 cup water
1 tablespoon soy sauce
2 teaspoons dry sherry
1 teaspoon instant chicken
  bouillon granules
8 green onions with tops
4 tablespoons vegetable oil,
  divided
3 stalks celery, diagonally cut
  into thin slices
1 can (8 ounces) water chestnuts,
  drained and cut into halves
1 can (8 ounces) sliced bamboo
  shoots, drained
8 ounces fresh *or* thawed frozen
  sea scallops, cut into quarters

1. Prepare Fried Noodles; set aside.

2. Peel shells from shrimp; discard shells. Remove veins from shrimp (page 210); set shrimp aside.

3. Remove skin from fish fillets; discard skin.

4. Cut fillets into 1 1/2-inch pieces; set aside.

5. Combine cornstarch, water, soy sauce, sherry and bouillon granules in small bowl; mix well. Set aside.

6. Diagonally cut green onions into thin slices.

7. Heat 2 tablespoons oil in wok or large skillet over high heat. Add green onions, celery, water chestnuts and bamboo shoots; stir-fry until crisp-tender, about 2 minutes. Remove from wok; set aside.

8. Heat remaining 2 tablespoons oil in wok over high heat. Add shrimp, fish pieces and scallops; stir-fry until all fish turns opaque and is cooked through, about 3 minutes.

9. Stir cornstarch mixture; add to wok. Cook and stir until sauce boils and thickens. Return vegetables to wok; cook and stir 2 minutes. Serve over Fried Noodles.　　*Makes 6 servings*

Step 2. Peeling shrimp.

Step 3. Removing skin from fish.

Step 6. Cutting onions.

Crab-Stuffed Shrimp

Sauce

2 tablespoons vegetable oil
1 small yellow onion, finely
   chopped
1 teaspoon curry powder
1½ tablespoons dry sherry
1 tablespoon satay sauce
2 teaspoons soy sauce
1 teaspoon sugar
¼ cup cream *or* milk

Shrimp

2 egg whites, lightly beaten
4 teaspoons cornstarch
1 tablespoon dry sherry
1 tablespoon soy sauce
2 cans (6½ ounces each)
   crabmeat, drained and flaked
8 green onions with tops, finely
   chopped
2 stalks celery, finely chopped
1½ pounds large shrimp, shelled
   and deveined
½ cup all-purpose flour
3 eggs
3 tablespoons milk
2 to 3 cups soft bread crumbs
   (from 8 to 10 bread slices)
Vegetable oil for frying

1. Heat 2 tablespoons oil in small saucepan over medium heat. Add yellow onion; cook and stir until tender, about 3 minutes. Add curry powder; cook and stir 1 minute. Add 1½ tablespoons sherry, satay sauce, 2 teaspoons soy sauce and sugar; cook and stir 2 minutes. Stir in cream; bring to a boil. Simmer 2 minutes, stirring occasionally. Keep warm.

2. Blend egg whites, cornstarch, 1 tablespoon sherry and 1 tablespoon soy sauce in medium bowl. Add crabmeat, green onions and celery; mix well.

3. Cut deep slit into, but not through, back of each shrimp.

4. Flatten shrimp slightly by pounding gently with mallet or rolling pin. Stuff crab mixture into slit of each shrimp.

5. Coat each shrimp lightly with flour.

6. Beat eggs and milk with fork in shallow bowl until blended. Place each shrimp, stuffed-side up, in egg mixture; spoon egg mixture over shrimp to coat completely.

7. Coat each shrimp with bread crumbs, pressing crumbs lightly onto shrimp. Place shrimp in single layer on cookie sheets or plates. Refrigerate 30 minutes.

8. Heat oil in wok or large skillet over high heat to 375°F. Add four or five shrimp at a time; cook until golden brown, about 3 minutes. Drain on paper towels. Serve with sauce.

Makes 4 servings

Step 3. Slitting back of shrimp.

Step 4. Stuffing shrimp.

Chinese Vegetables

2 medium yellow onions
1 pound fresh broccoli*
8 ounces fresh snow peas *or*
    1 package (6 ounces) thawed
    frozen snow peas*
3/4 cup water
1 tablespoon instant chicken
    bouillon granules
2 tablespoons vegetable oil
1 tablespoon minced fresh ginger
8 ounces fresh spinach,* coarsely
    chopped
4 stalks celery,* diagonally cut
    into 1/2-inch pieces
8 green onions with tops,*
    diagonally cut into thin slices

*Or, use sliced carrots, zucchini, green
beans or green peppers in addition to, or
in place of, the listed vegetables.

1. Cut yellow onions into eight wedges; separate layers (page 202).

2. Trim woody stems from broccoli; discard.

3. Cut broccoli tops into florets.

4. Cut larger florets and stalks into $2 \times 1/4$-inch strips; set aside.

5. Trim snow peas and remove strings; set aside.

6. Combine water and bouillon granules in small bowl; mix well. Set aside.

7. Heat oil in wok or large skillet over high heat. Add yellow onions, broccoli strips and ginger; stir-fry 1 minute. Add broccoli florets, snow peas, spinach, celery and green onions; toss lightly.

8. Add bouillon mixture; mix lightly until vegetables are well coated. Bring to a boil; cover. Cook until vegetables are crisp-tender, 2 to 3 minutes. *Makes 4 to 6 servings*

Step 3. Cutting broccoli into florets.

Step 4. Cutting larger florets and stalks into strips.

Step 5. Trimming snow peas.

Zucchini Shanghai Style

4 dried mushrooms
  Water
1 large tomato
½ cup chicken broth
2 tablespoons ketchup
2 teaspoons soy sauce
1 teaspoon dry sherry
¼ teaspoon sugar
⅛ teaspoon salt
1 teaspoon red wine vinegar
1 teaspoon cornstarch
2 tablespoons vegetable oil,
    divided
1 teaspoon minced fresh ginger
1 clove garlic, minced
1 green onion with top, finely
    chopped
1 pound zucchini, diagonally cut
    into 1-inch pieces
½ small yellow onion, cut into
    wedges and separated

1. Place mushrooms in small bowl; add enough warm water to cover mushrooms completely. Let stand 30 minutes. Drain, reserving ¼ cup liquid. Squeeze out excess water.

2. Cut stems off mushrooms; discard. Cut caps into thin slices.

3. To loosen skin from tomato, add tomato to small saucepan of boiling water. Let stand 30 to 45 seconds. Rinse immediately under cold running water. Gently peel skin from tomato.

4. Cut tomato in half. Remove stem and seeds; discard.

5. Coarsely chop tomato; set aside.

6. Combine reserved ¼ cup mushroom liquid, chicken broth, ketchup, soy sauce, sherry, sugar, salt and vinegar in small bowl; set aside.

7. Combine cornstarch and 1 tablespoon water in small cup; mix well. Set aside.

8. Heat 1 tablespoon oil in wok or large skillet over medium-high heat. Add ginger and garlic; stir-fry 10 seconds. Add mushrooms, tomato and green onion; stir-fry 1 minute. Stir in chicken broth mixture. Bring to a boil. Reduce heat to low; simmer 10 minutes, stirring occasionally. Remove from wok; set aside.

9. Add remaining 1 tablespoon oil to wok; heat over medium-high heat. Add zucchini and yellow onion; stir-fry 30 seconds. Add 3 tablespoons water; cover. Cook, stirring occasionally, until vegetables are crisp-tender, 3 to 4 minutes. Stir cornstarch mixture. Add to wok with mushroom mixture. Cook and stir until sauce boils and thickens.

Makes 4 to 6 servings

Step 3. Peeling tomato.

Step 4. Removing tomato seeds.

Ma Po Bean Curd

**1 tablespoon Szechuan
    peppercorns* (optional)**
12 to 14 ounces bean curd, drained
³/₄ cup chicken broth
1 tablespoon soy sauce
1 tablespoon dry sherry
1¹/₂ tablespoons cornstarch
3 tablespoons water
2 tablespoons vegetable oil
4 ounces lean ground pork
2 teaspoons minced fresh ginger
2 cloves garlic, minced
1 tablespoon hot bean sauce
**2 green onions with tops, thinly
    sliced**
1 teaspoon sesame oil
    Fresh chives for garnish

*Szechuan peppercorns are deceptively
potent. Wear rubber or plastic gloves
when crushing them and do not touch
eyes or lips when handling.

1. Place peppercorns in small dry skillet.
Cook and stir over medium-low heat until
fragrant, about 2 minutes; let cool.

2. Place peppercorns between paper towels;
crush with hammer. Set aside.

3. Cut bean curd into ¹/₂-inch cubes. Set aside.

4. Combine chicken broth, soy sauce and
sherry in small bowl; set aside. Combine
cornstarch and water in small cup; mix well.
Set aside.

5. Heat vegetable oil in wok or large skillet
over high heat. Add meat; stir-fry until no
longer pink, about 2 minutes. Add ginger,
garlic and hot bean sauce. Stir-fry until meat
absorbs color from bean sauce, about 1
minute.

6. Add chicken broth mixture and bean curd;
simmer, uncovered, 5 minutes. Stir in onions.
Stir cornstarch mixture; add to wok. Cook
until sauce boils and thickens slightly, stirring
constantly. Stir in sesame oil. Sprinkle with
ground peppercorns and garnish, if desired.

Makes 3 to 4 servings

Step 1. Cooking peppercorns.

Step 2. Crushing peppercorns.

Step 3. Cutting bean curd into
cubes.

Chinese Mixed Pickled Vegetables

Pickling Liquid
 3 cups sugar
 3 cups distilled white vinegar
 1^1/$_2$ cups water
 1^1/$_2$ teaspoons salt

Vegetables
 1 large Chinese white radish
  (about 1 pound)
 3 large carrots
 1 large cucumber, seeded
  (page 188)
 4 stalks celery, diagonally cut
  into ^{1}/$_2$-inch pieces
 8 green onions, diagonally cut
  into ^{1}/$_4$-inch pieces
 1 large red pepper, cut into
  ^{1}/$_2$-inch pieces
 1 large green pepper, cut into
  ^{1}/$_2$-inch pieces
 4 ounces fresh ginger, peeled and
  thinly sliced
  Green Onion Curls for garnish
  (page 170)

1. Combine all pickling liquid ingredients in 3-quart saucepan. Bring to a boil over medium heat, stirring occasionally. Cool.

2. Cut radish into matchstick pieces. Repeat with carrots and cucumber.

3. Fill large saucepan or Dutch oven ^{1}/$_2$ full with water. Bring to a boil. Add radish, carrots, cucumber, celery, onions, red pepper, green pepper and ginger. Remove from heat. Let stand 2 minutes.

4. Drain vegetables in large colander. Spread vegetables out onto clean towels; allow to dry 2 to 3 hours.

5. Pack vegetables firmly into clean jars with tight-fitting lids. Pour Pickling Liquid into jars to cover vegetables. Seal jars tightly. Store in refrigerator at least 1 week before using. Serve garnished, if desired.

Makes 1^1/$_2$ to 2 quarts

Step 2. Cutting radish.

Step 4. Drying cooked vegetables.

Step 5. Covering vegetables with Pickling Liquid.

Fried Rice

3 cups water
1¹/₂ teaspoons salt
1¹/₂ cups uncooked long-grain rice
4 slices uncooked bacon, chopped
3 eggs
¹/₈ teaspoon pepper
2 tablespoons *plus* 3 teaspoons
  vegetable oil, divided
2 teaspoons minced fresh ginger
8 ounces Barbecued Pork
  (page 170), cut into thin strips
8 ounces shelled deveined shrimp
  (page 210), cooked and
  coarsely chopped
8 green onions with tops, finely
  chopped
1 to 2 tablespoons soy sauce
  Fresh chervil leaves for garnish

1. Combine water and salt in 3-quart saucepan; cover. Bring to a boil over medium-high heat. Stir in rice. Reduce heat to low; cover. Simmer until rice is tender, 15 to 20 minutes; drain.

2. Cook bacon in wok or large skillet over medium heat, stirring frequently, until crisp; drain.

3. Remove all but 1 tablespoon bacon drippings from wok.

4. Beat eggs with pepper in small bowl. Pour ¹/₃ of egg mixture into wok, tilting wok slightly to cover bottom.

5. Cook over medium heat until eggs are set, 1 to 2 minutes. Remove from wok.

6. Roll up omelet; cut into thin strips.

7. Pour 1¹/₂ teaspoons oil into wok. Add ¹/₂ of remaining egg mixture, tilting wok to cover bottom. Cook until eggs are set. Remove from wok; roll up and cut into thin strips. Repeat with another 1¹/₂ teaspoons oil and remaining eggs.

8. Heat remaining 2 tablespoons oil in wok over medium-high heat. Add ginger; stir-fry 1 minute. Add rice; cook 5 minutes, stirring frequently. Stir in omelet strips, bacon, Barbecued Pork, shrimp, onions and soy sauce. Cook and stir until heated through. Garnish, if desired.

Makes 6 to 8 servings

Step 2. Cooking bacon.

Step 4. Tilting wok to cover bottom with egg mixture.

Step 6. Cutting omelet into strips.

Cold Stirred Noodles

Dressing

  6 tablespoons soy sauce
  2 tablespoons sesame oil
  ¼ cup red wine vinegar
  2½ tablespoons sugar
  ¼ to ½ teaspoon chili oil

Noodles

  1 pound Chinese-style thin egg
    noodles
  1 tablespoon sesame oil
  ½ large thin-skinned cucumber
  2 small carrots
  1 bunch radishes
  3 cups bean sprouts
  1 cup matchstick strips
    Barbecued Pork (page 170),
    optional
  4 green onions with tops, cut into
    2-inch slivers
  Thin cucumber slices for
    garnish

1. For dressing, combine soy sauce, 2 tablespoons sesame oil, vinegar, sugar and chili oil in small bowl; mix well.

2. Cut noodles into 6-inch pieces.

3. Cook noodles according to package directions until tender but still firm, 2 to 3 minutes; drain. Rinse under cold running water; drain again.

4. Combine noodles and 1 tablespoon sesame oil; toss lightly to coat. Refrigerate until ready to serve.

5. Cut cucumber into 3-inch pieces. Shred with hand shredder or food processor; set aside. Repeat with carrots. Shred radishes; set aside.

6. Add carrots to saucepan of boiling water; cook 30 seconds. Drain. Rinse under cold running water; drain again. Repeat with bean sprouts.

7. To serve, place noodles on large platter. Top with shredded cucumber, carrots, bean sprouts, radishes and Barbecued Pork; sprinkle with onions. Garnish, if desired. Serve with dressing.　　*Makes 6 to 8 servings*

Step 2. Cutting noodles.

Step 5. Shredding cucumber.

Step 6. Cooking bean sprouts.

Fried Noodles

8 ounces Chinese-style thin egg
   noodles
Vegetable oil for frying

1. Cook noodles according to package directions until tender but still firm, 2 to 3 minutes; drain. Rinse under cold running water; drain again.

2. Place several layers of paper towels over jelly-roll pans or cookie sheets. Spread noodles over paper towels; let dry 2 to 3 hours.

3. Heat about 2 inches oil in wok or large skillet over medium-high heat to 375°F. Using slotted spoon or tongs, lower a small portion of noodles into hot oil. Cook noodles until golden brown, about 30 seconds.

4. Drain noodles on paper towels. Repeat with remaining noodles. *Makes 4 servings*

Step 3. Frying noodles.

Step 4. Draining cooked noodles.

Steamed Rice

1 cup uncooked long-grain rice
2 cups water
1 tablespoon oil
1 teaspoon salt

1. Place rice in strainer; rinse under cold running water to remove excess starch. Combine rice, 2 cups water, oil and salt in medium saucepan.

2. Cook over medium-high heat until water comes to a boil. Reduce heat to low; cover. Simmer until rice is tender, 15 to 20 minutes. Remove from heat; let stand 5 minutes. Uncover; fluff rice lightly with fork. *Makes 3 cups*

Step 2. Fluffing rice.

Vermicelli

8 ounces Chinese rice vermicelli
***or* bean threads**
Vegetable oil for frying

1. Cut bundle of vermicelli in half. Gently pull each half apart into small bunches.

2. Heat about 2 inches oil in wok or large skillet over medium-high heat to 375°F. Using slotted spoon or tongs, lower a small bunch of vermicelli into hot oil.

3. Cook until vermicelli rises to top, 3 to 5 seconds; remove immediately.

4. Drain vermicelli on paper towels. Repeat with remaining vermicelli.

Makes about 4 servings

Step 1. Separating vermicelli.

Step 2. Adding vermicelli to hot oil.

Step 3. Cooking vermicelli.

INDEX

METRIC CONVERSION CHART

VOLUME MEASUREMENT (dry)

⅛ teaspoon = .5 mL
¼ teaspoon = 1 mL
½ teaspoon = 2 mL
¾ teaspoon = 4 mL
1 teaspoon = 5 mL
1 tablespoon = 15 mL
2 tablespoons = 25 mL
¼ cup = 50 mL
⅓ cup = 75 mL
⅔ cup = 150 mL
¾ cup = 175 mL
1 cup = 250 mL
2 cups = 1 pint = 500 mL
3 cups = 750 mL
4 cups = 1 quart = 1 L

VOLUME MEASUREMENT (fluid)

1 fluid ounce (2 tablespoons) = 30 mL
4 fluid ounces (½ cup) = 125 mL
8 fluid ounces (1 cup) = 250 mL
12 fluid ounces (1½ cups) = 375 mL
16 fluid ounces (2 cups) = 500 mL

WEIGHT (mass)

½ ounce = 15 g
1 ounce = 30 g
3 ounces = 85 g
3.75 ounces = 100 g
4 ounces = 115 g
8 ounces = 225 g
12 ounces = 340 g
16 ounces = 1 pound = 450 g

DIMENSION

1/16 inch = 2 mm
⅛ inch = 3 mm
¼ inch = 6 mm
½ inch = 1.5 cm
¾ inch = 2 cm
1 inch = 2.5 cm

OVEN TEMPERATURE

250°F = 120°C
275°F = 140°C
300°F = 150°C
325°F = 160°C
350°F = 180°C
375°F = 190°C
400°F = 200°C
425°F = 220°C
450°F = 230°C

BAKING PAN SIZE

Utensil	Size in Inches/Quarts	Metric Volume	Size in Centimeters
Baking or	8 × 8 × 2	2 L	20 × 20 × 5
Cake pan	9 × 9 × 2	2.5 L	22 × 22 × 5
(square or	12 × 8 × 2	3 L	30 × 20 × 5
rectangular)	13 × 9 × 2	3.5 L	33 × 23 × 5
Loaf Pan	8 × 4 × 3	1.5 L	20 × 10 × 7
	9 × 5 × 3	2 L	23 × 13 × 7
Round Layer	8 × 1½	1.2 L	20 × 4
Cake Pan	9 × 1½	1.5 L	23 × 4
Pie Plate	8 × 1¼	750 mL	20 × 3
	9 × 1¼	1 L	23 × 3
Baking Dish	1 quart	1 L	
or Casserole	1½ quart	1.5 L	
	2 quart	2 L	